Winning Races

All you need to know to improve your yacht's performance

John Heyes

ADLARD COLES NAUTICAL
London

Contents

Acknowledgements

I would like to thank the many friends in the yacht racing business who have so kindly offered their advice and specialist expertise. In particular, Ian Ridge for the lessons in fairing hulls and keels and Peter Kay for advice on sails and sail fabrics.

Paul Pritchard has sailed with us as tactician on many occasions and I am indebted to him for reading the manuscript and for his invaluable input to the tactical chapters.

Finally I have to thank the publisher for her great patience in awaiting the manuscript.

JOHN HEYES, 1995

Photos by the author and diagrams by J C Winters unless otherwise credited.

The following registered trade names belong to the owners detailed below. The absence of a ® mark next to each individual entry does not imply any lack of recognition of the validity of these marks on the part of the publisher or the author.

KEVLAR® is produced exclusively by Dupont, USA
SPECTRA® is produced exclusively by Allied, USA
DYNEEMA® is produced exclusively by DSM, Holland
VECTRAN® is produced exclusively by Hoechst Celanese, USA
TWARON® is produced exclusively by Akzo Nobel, Germany
TECHNORA® is produced exclusively by Teijin, Japan

Published by Adlard Coles Nautical 1995
an imprint of A & C Black (Publishers) Ltd
35 Bedford Row, London WC1R 4JH

Copyright © John Heyes 1995

ISBN 0-7136-3862-1

A CIP catalogue record for this book is available from the British Library.

Typeset in 10 on 12 pt Photina by
Falcon Oast Graphic Art
Printed and bound in Great Britain by
The Cromwell Press, Melksham, Wiltshire

Part 1: BOATSPEED

1. Who Needs This Book?

The sport of yacht racing is changing. Apart from the more obvious aspects such as the growth of IMS type boats, the format of racing at the Olympics or the sudden arrival of boats with bow-sprits, more subtle and less apparent changes are taking place.

For those of us that spend our weekends racing keelboats and cruiser racers, the technology now found aboard has come a long way in the last few years. Laminate mylar sails are no longer penalised under the Channel Handicap System (CHS) and are commonplace amongst the fleet. Keener racers now opt for Kevlar or similar hi-tech fabric sails, whilst down below and up on deck instruments abound. GPS and Decca make sextants museum exhibits. The course for the weekend Channel race can be input to the yacht's PC from the comfort of the armchair at home, or more likely in the office on a Friday afternoon. There is now a bewildering variety of deck gear, winches and layout options to choose from when fitting out or re-vamping your boat. And keels no longer look like they used to either!

The sailors themselves are changing too. They are now a much more transient bunch, moving from boat to boat, class to class, and from dinghies to yachts, all within the same season. It is not uncommon for dinghy sailors to take in two or three national championships and then jump on a big boat for a regatta such as Cowes Week or Cork Week. The top racers are now perceived as those that can win in almost any type of boat. In the last couple of years, Laurie Smith has gone from skippering an Admiral's Cup One Tonner, to a Whitbread 60, then on to Olympic Soling campaign and just found time to win the Ultra 30 circuit during his week-ends off. No longer do you have to spend years sailing in the same fleet before you gain the respect of the class elders; it is now more a question of the size, spread and results on your sailing CV.

However, this increase in the mobility of sailors creates new problems in yacht racing. Where does the keen dinghy or keelboat sailor acquire the necessary skills and knowledge to make the transfer from small to big boat? Where do yacht racers turn to improve their knowledge and boat perform-ance? The problem is the same right across the sport. Literally within months of returning from the Games, Olympic sailors around the world have found themselves driving Admirals Cup, America's Cup and Whitbread boats. At the other end of the spectrum, the club dinghy ace is often asked to helm a friend's keelboat in the local area championship and goes on from there to become involved in cruiser racer events. But where does, say, the Finn or Laser sailor learn how to steer with a wheel, operate a GPS, gybe a big boat spinnaker, make a headsail change and perform countless other manoeuvres he has never met before? Similarly a one-design keelboat racer moving up to a bigger race boat will find that it takes the closely coordinated efforts of five crew to gybe the spinnaker and that a laminate mainsail has to be set up in a different way from its Dacron relation.

Historically yacht crews served their time on the rail before being offered a position of responsibility on board. This provided the aspiring crew ample time to see how manoeuvres were carried out and how the team as a whole worked. But as the equipment and techniques involved in sail trim and rig tune become so much more technical, each crew job becomes more specialised and individual. These days a mainsail trimmer would be lost forward of the mast and likewise a bowman is never allowed near the cockpit, so specialised has the art of crew work become. Nowadays you need to study and build up the necessary skills for each different position on the boat. The great problem is that there is often no one available or perhaps even capable of training the novice sail trimmer. There is rarely room for two mainsheet trimmers to sit together in the cockpit and discuss mainsail trim, so how can you learn what you are supposed to do when given the mainsheet of a 40 footer for the first time in your life?

I can remember asking an up and coming young helmsman how he had made the jump from being a champion dinghy sailor to being asked to drive large race boats. After early success in a couple of J24 regattas he had suddenly been asked if he could helm a Swan in their World Championships in Sardinia. Rashly accepting the invitation he arrived on the dock never having sailed a boat with a wheel before in his life. His advice was to be vague about actual previous experience and pick it up as you go along! This may be fine if you have great natural ability as a helmsman, but in other positions on the boat some previous knowledge of techniques and manoeuvres is vital if you don't want to look stupid on your first outing.

I hate to admit that on my very first time aboard a yacht in an offshore race, I did just that. It was on a long run back from the Nab Tower up the Solent when the wind dropped and the skipper called for the lazy guy to be removed from the clew of the kite to lighten the weight on the sail; a simple enough job. Being the keen new boy I volunteered and rushed forward to the foredeck. Attached to the clew I found a bewildering variety of snap shackles, swivels and rings. Not sure which one to release, I looked back for some advice, but none of the crew was bothering to watch such an obvious job. Not wishing to expose my inexperience, I fired off the larger of the two snap shackles and then watched in horror as the clew of the spinnaker blew gently forward, completely free of any sheet. I had chosen the wrong shackle! Luckily the wind was light enough for the bowman to grasp the clew and quickly re-connect the single sheet – and the crew laid back enough to forgive my mistake.

The aim of this book is to help speed up the learning curve for the sailor keen to improve but short on experience. If you race on the same boat and at the same level all the time, it is very hard to improve or learn anything new.

In any class or fleet you often come across older, highly experienced sailors who, say, ten years ago were regularly in the top three at major championships but now are somehow always relegated to mid-fleet. I often wondered why this was. You cannot 'unlearn' sailing; it is much like riding a bike. The more you do the greater the all important experience. The answer is that fleets become more competitive as the hulls, rigs, sails, and even styles of sailing the boats are updated and refined.

True, you can improve boatspeed by buying better sails or spars, but the better the equipment performs, the more care, attention and knowledge are required to set it up correctly in order to achieve the extra gain in performance. So if you carry on sailing the boat the same way as you have for years, it is no wonder that others are slowly going past you.

Similarly techniques of racing the boats are changing too. As an example, when I began crewing in the Dragon class some fourteen years ago, the boat was sailed by the owner who helmed, did all the tactics, called sail trim and barked orders at the two crew who were just there to tack and gybe the boat when required. These days the Dragon is raced very much as an equal three-man (three persons in many cases) team. In the front is the genoa trimmer, able to fine tune the sail, control mast bend, call changes in wind and waves, monitor the boat's relative speed and is also responsible for any foredeck work necessary. The middleman is the tactician and boatspeed guru. He or she calls the shots, laylines, when to sail 'fat' (low and free), and when to squeeze high as the tactics dictate. In charge of general boatspeed and mainsail trim in particular, the middleman will also take the spinnaker sheets downwind. The helmsman is possibly the least important crew member, but requires strong powers of concentration and natural feel to keep the boat at maximum speed through the waves. The Dragon has a full bow and is slow to accelerate, so steering through a short chop in little wind calls for 100 per cent concentration, powerful sails and good technique on the helm. Helmsmen may contribute to tactics when they have time to look up, depending on conditions at the time. They are also responsible for close quarters positioning (such as at starts and mark roundings) when reactions and decisions have to be instant.

The modern day owner may be found in any one of these three positions, or even watching from ashore. This may be over stating the case, but it serves to illustrate how the game changes over time. Interestingly, six years on in the Dragon class, even the most vociferous of the old school who complained about the appearance of 'professional' tacticians in the boat can now be seen sailing with acknowledged experts amongst their crew.

Sailing is one of the few sports where women can take on men on an equal footing. Cathy Foster won the last race of the 1984 Olympic 470 regatta as the only female in the fleet, and an all-women crew sailed *America 3* to second place in the 1994 IACC World Championship, ahead of Dennis Conner. So wherever the text in this book refers to 'him', bowman, or helmsman, please take it to refer equally to either male or female crew.

Only by sailing in a variety of different boats and fleets and – more importantly – with sailors more experienced than yourself, will your own game improve. At the same time you have to want to learn and be prepared to do a bit of studying. Don't sit back on the rail when a top tactician comes on board and guides you faultlessly up the beat without quizzing him afterwards about why he chose the righthand side, and how did he know the new wind would come in along the shore first? You have to want to know the answers.

Hopefully, this book will, spark off ideas and draw to your attention areas of your boat's performance which are not as hot as they could be. Is the deck layout completely workable? When was the last time you looked at the mast set up? Maybe you should spend time recalibrating the instruments?

Winning Races is written for sailors who have been racing for some time and are now ready to make their impression on the front of the fleet. To do so requires first of all an ability to prioritise those areas of the race that need improving first. Buying the best new sails will not get you to the windward mark first if your boat handling is still appalling or if the mast is not set up right. It is, of course, hard to work out why you were slow in the last race and hence which areas you need to work on first. Was the boat slower than the competition when the breeze got up because the mast was falling off too much, or was the genoa out of its range, or were you just sailing in more foul tide than the others? This is where yacht racing becomes a detective game and a sharp analytical mind is required. Solving specific boatspeed problems can sometimes be a matter of trial and error, but hopefully this book will shorten the time taken and even save unnecessary expense.

No book can replace the experience gained from hours on the water. However, those hours afloat can be maximised if backed up by a little off-the-water research and reading. Sailmakers' seminars, navigation lectures, or just a beer with competitors after the race are all great opportunities to learn why one boat won the race and others did not. Now and again you may have to be prepared to alter your opinion of how, say, a spinnaker should be trimmed in light air. Occasionally techniques which work well on one boat will not be so fast on a different type of rig. Develop an open and enquiring approach to your sailing. As the standing joke on our boat goes whenever someone fouls up. 'Try to develop a feel for the sport!'

As your skills and experience develop, so confidence in your abilities will grow. With this new confidence comes a dramatic jump in performance, and this is mainly what I believe separates the good sailors from the great. If you have the confidence that your trim and tactics are right, you do not waste time with negative thoughts and are quicker and more settled when making decisions. Winning comes easier with confidence.

2. Preparing the Boat

As any racing fleet becomes more popular the competition increases and so crews start thinking about their boats, wondering what can be done to make them go faster. A common story is that of a keen newcomer joining a fleet with an established pecking order, in a well prepared boat. He soon starts winning races and as a result his boat is subject to the closest scrutiny by the rest of the fleet. Once the more competitive members of the class or fleet have seen and accepted that fairing the keel, adding more rake, using more rig tension or whatever changes our new boy has been actually makes the boat go faster, they begin to follow suit. As soon as other boats' performance is seen to improve everyone is doing it, and so the whole performance of the fleet is raised.

But what if your boat is a one-design and you are not allowed to do much to it? It is true to say that the more restrictive the class rules, the greater the relative effect of any improvements you can make to the standard finish or set up. Assuming you have just taken delivery of a second-hand or even new yacht, where do you start to make the boat go faster?

Fairing the hull

Obviously all the underwater surfaces should be as smooth and as fair as possible and certainly as good as, if not better, than the competition's. A complete re-fairing is a major undertaking but should not be necessary for production boats built in a female mould. To check the fairness of your hull use a three metre length of hard wood batten held against the hull, parallel to the waterline. Sight along the batten to see if it touches the hull for its entire length. Ring any low areas with a marker pen as you go, so that once the whole of the underwater area has been profiled in this way the extent of any un-fairness will be evident. Now you can decide if the condition of the hull is bad enough to warrant an all over re-fairing or if a localised area only needs to be done.

The trick for fairing any area of the hull is to use as long a sanding board as possible, so that any hollows are bridged. A small sanding block will simply follow the existing contours of the hull, deepening any lows. If large areas are to be rubbed down and four pairs of hands are available, a three metre length of standard 65 mm plastic rainwater pipe is often the best tool. Start by glueing a long strip of 80 grit paper (available in rolls,

Fairing the hull with a length of plastic pipe.

110 mm wide) on to the pipe. Then with four people, with hands equally spaced, wrap the pipe around the hull at 45° to the keel and start to sand (see photo above).

Clearly the fairing team need to carefully co-ordinate their efforts and maintain an equal pressure on the pipe. In order to sand to a consistent depth across the hull count the strokes as the pipe moves over the first area, working from the boot-top down towards the centreline. After 20 strokes move the pipe along the boat a third of the pipe length and count another 20 strokes, following the same angle as before. Once the end of the boat is reached, work your way back along the hull, but this time using the pipe in the other 45°orientation to the keel (see Fig 2.1). Finish off this initial sanding with a pass along the hull, parallel to the keel (ie, with the pipe at right angles to the waterline). The objective of all this rubbing down is to remove the high areas to expose the lows. Any lows remaining can now be filled with a mixture of epoxy resin and micro ballons. If there is a significant depth of filler to apply, mix in some Colloidal Silica to make a more thixotropic mix, which is easier to apply and will not run. There are also special low-density fillers available, which are easier to sand down, but be careful that the hull's strength is not compromised and that the resulting texture is sufficiently smooth.

The whole rubbing down process now has to be repeated with 120 grit, until you are satisfied that the hull is as fair as you can get it. The next stage is to paint on – or much better to spray on – an epoxy hi-build paint, such as Awlgrip's fairing compound, to achieve an even coverage of up to 2 mm if necessary. Once rubbed down again with a 240 grit you need to apply an epoxy primer before spraying on the top coat of either antifouling or a two pot polyurethane paint. It is vital to protect the hull with a sufficient thickness of epoxy as you will have removed most of the original gel-coat layer with the initial sanding.

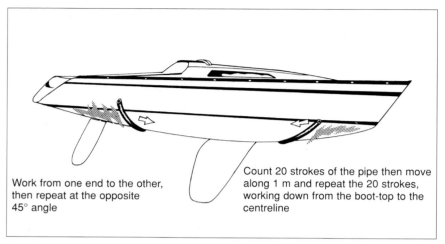

Work from one end to the other, then repeat at the opposite 45° angle

Count 20 strokes of the pipe then move along 1 m and repeat the 20 strokes, working down from the boot-top to the centreline

Fig 2.1 *Fairing the hull with a 3 m length of 65 mm plastic pipe.*

If all this sounds like too much hard work, find a boatyard that specialises in fairing race boats and pay the money! If done well the finished job should add value to your boat, protect it from osmosis, as well as make it go faster. If your budget or time is limited, it is more important in terms of boatspeed gains to concentrate your efforts on the keel and rudder.

Checking the keel and rudder

Before looking at the shape of the keel it is vital to check that both the rudder and keel are on straight and are in line with each other. You would be amazed how many yachts have keels which are slightly out of alignment, either because the boat has taken the ground hard at some stage, or because the keel was not bolted on straight in the first place. A further factor with boats which are trailed long distances can be movement of the keel caused by the constant pounding and vibration. Ensure the trailer supports the hull equally and that not all the weight is taken on the keel. (However, do not go to the other extreme, as support pads can indent the hull if not placed in the right reinforced areas, or if they take too much of the load.) If towing over long distances you need a trailer with the best suspension you can afford to avoid damaging the hull.

Increasingly imported boats get shipped in with the keel and rudder removed to reduce transport costs. When the keel is bolted on it may be necessary to pack the top plate on one side to get the keel absolutely vertical.

Aligning the foils

In order to ascertain if the keel and rudder are in line, it is first necessary to level the boat up on its cradle. To do this make yourself a simple manometer level from a length of clear plastic tube. Tie the tube up either side of the boat and fill it with water until the water comes near the top of the toe rail or other suitable measurement reference point. Level up the boat by jacking up the cradle until the measurement stations on either side match the water level in the tube. Next drop a plumb bob from the bow to set up a vertical reference. Sight the rudder and keel in line with the string from a boat length or so away from both the forward and aft ends. If there is any disparity between the alignment of the foils check each in turn by sighting in line with the plumb, in order to see which appendage is vertical to the hull and which one is out of line. Occasionally a keel may be twisted, so drop a second plumb line behind the keel, perhaps off the p-bracket, to see if the trailing edge lines up.

If you find that the keel is not exactly in line don't panic! It is a relatively painless affair to put right, as long as you can loosen off the keel-bolts. If you do have to move the keel, it is worth a careful study of the class rules (in the case of a one-design class) to ensure your keel is of maximum depth and suitably raked, as either of these aspects may be easily altered at this stage. In the case of the J-24 class, the 'fast' position for the keel is as far forward as allowed and maximum chord length.

To straighten up a keel first loosen off the bolts so that the keel is free to move. With the hull level clamp or fix the keel in a vertical position, using the aft plumb line to line up the trailing edge. When you are happy that the keel is straight measure the gap each side between the bottom of the hull and the top of the keel. This measurement will tell you the depth of the fillet required between keel and hull to make the keel sit vertically. With the keel held firmly, slack the keelbolts off further and jack the boat up slightly away from the keel. Fill the top of the keel plate with an epoxy 'bog', of resin and Colloidal Silica, to the required depth and leave it to go off hard. Later, tighten the keelbolts down on to the epoxy and finish off by fairing in the join line.

If your inspection reveals that it is the rudder which is out of line the best solution is to adjust one of the rudder bearings. The top bearing is generally the easiest to get to, often being screwed into the deck. Simply move the bearing until the rudder blade comes into line with the keel. Check that the cause of the problem is not just excessive wear in the bearings and that no anti-fouling has found its way on to the bearing surfaces.

Keel shape

The shape of the keel and the area of the hull directly in front of it are the most critical underwater surfaces affecting boatspeed. Just as with the sail, the leading edge of both foils needs to be fair and smooth in order to keep the flow attached as far aft as possible. A yacht's keel will commonly have its maximum depth further forward than that of a sail, at around 30%. This draft forward shape creates a more efficient lift to drag ratio at the relatively slow speeds of say 6.5 knots at which it sails upwind. A mainsail, in comparison, is likely to have a maximum depth at 50% back from the leading edge (known as the draft position) and can experience wind speeds of anything from 5 to 35 knots. It is no surprise therefore to find that high speed sailing boats such as planning dinghies and catamarans have foils with the draft at closer to 35% aft, rather than 30%.

The area at the front of the keel is vital to maintaining attached flow over the keel. Any rough spots here will cause separated flow, which breaks away early from the foil, creating large turbulent eddies, otherwise

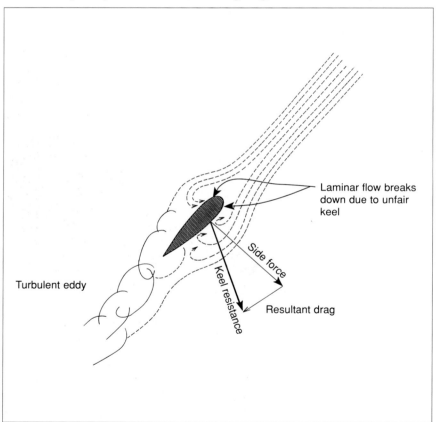

Fig 2.2 *The water flow around an unfair keel will create turbulence and results in the breakdown of laminar flow. The side forces then increase and the boat makes more leeway. If one side of the keel is thicker than the other, more lift will be generated on one tack than the other.*

known as drag. If the turbulent flow is sufficient and flow over the keel breaks down no lift is produced and the foil becomes stalled. As a result the boat slides to leeward (see Fig. 2.2).

Race boats which are dry-sailed occasionally suffer damage in this important area from dirty or worn lifting slings which cut into the forward edge of the keel when the boat is being launched. So if you only ever see your boat in the water ready for the weekend race, arrange to inspect the hull out of the water regularly through the season, and especially before a major regatta.

Another common cause of un-fairness in the critical pre-keel zone can occur if the boat was laid-up in a mould made in two halves and joined along the centreline. There may be a slight ridge left along the join line and down the leading edge of the keel which should be faired out.

Fairing a keel or rudder

The amount of work you choose to carry out on the rudder an keel will clearly depend on their current condition but also on the rules governing the boat. International one-design classes such as the J-24 and the Mumm 36 have a table of offsets printed in the class rules, from which you can make your own set of templates to check the foils are the right shape. The

Sight the rudder and keel to check they are correctly aligned. Hang a plumb line off the bow and stern as a sight line.

class Chief Measurer will have an official set of aluminium templates which it may be possible to borrow. National one-design classes such as the Sigma 38 in the UK often have less restrictive rules which allow 'filling and fairing to remove minor casting blemishes, as long as the keel profile is not altered from standard'. You may wish to optimise the keel shape and position by taking advantage of any beneficial measurement tolerances written into the rules if there is sufficient margin.

Rather than re-shaping the keel to a perfect NACA wing section, a more realistic goal is simply to end up with a fair and symmetrical keel. The 'in's and out's' of which keel section is fastest for your boat is best left to the designer, and will always be a compromise between upwind and down-wind performance. Do not be surprised if your keel is not symmetrical. The J-24 keel, for instance, is invariably thicker one side than the other at the top. This is a product of the recent trend for production boatbuilders to encapsulate the lead keel in a GRP 'shoe' so that the laborious filling and sanding stage is eliminated. However, in practice the glue used to bond the keel to the shoe gets pushed out to the top of the keel unevenly and can distort the thin glass shoe, resulting in one side of the keel being thicker than the other.

The first stage in making a keel symmetrical is first to find the thickest side and then build up the other side to match, as it is easier to add epoxy than to remove it. If the boat is a custom design or there are no keel templates available, you will need to make a set of templates from this chosen side.

Making a keel template

The first stage is to carefully draw on the centreline of the keel down the forward and aft edges. Next mark on the waterline sections, 150–250 mm apart, which will be the positions for the templates. To begin shaping the template, take some thick card or thin 4 mm ply and roughly cut a template to fit each section; just accurate to within 30 mm of the keel. The next stage may require a couple of pairs of helping hands, as you have to find some way of holding the rough template horizontally on station against the keel. A couple of 100 × 50 mm timbers are ideal, the ends of which, held level at each waterline section, will serve as a base to rest the card on and should prevent it from moving whilst you work on it. Accurately mark the centreline at the forward and aft edges and then 'spile' around the keel using a 30 mm spacer block to trace a profile of the keel section on to the card (Fig 2.3). Then take the card pattern and place it on top of a piece of good quality 10 mm ply (which is to be the finished template). Using a pin or spike, prick through the card pattern to transfer the profile on to the ply beneath, remembering to include the two centre-line reference marks. Using the same spacer block in reverse, transfer the marks and width of the block back towards the centreline to gain an

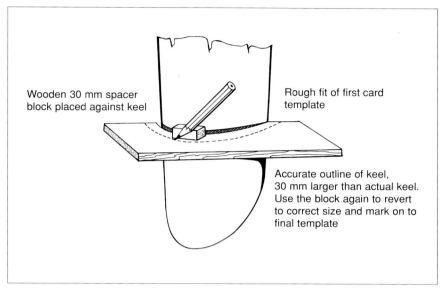

Wooden 30 mm spacer block placed against keel

Rough fit of first card template

Accurate outline of keel, 30 mm larger than actual keel. Use the block again to revert to correct size and mark on to final template

Fig 2.3 *Marking a keel template.*

accurate representation of the shape of the keel. Fair through the marks on the ply with a batten to complete the shape of the section. If the process is repeated for the other side of the keel and also drawn on to the same piece of plywood, symmetrically opposite, you then have an accurate drawing of that particular waterline section.

If you were previously unsure as to which was the thickest side of the keel, it is now possible to measure the maximum depth, relative to the centreline on both sides of the keel to check if one side is different from the other. In the case of J-24 keels it is not uncommon to find differences of up to 15 mm. This means that one side of the keel is contributing more lift than the other, so making more leeway on one tack than the other, all the way around the course and every time you go sailing. Put like that you can see why it is worth trying to make the appendages symmetrical.

Having decided which side of the keel has the greatest depth, make templates for each waterline section. Cut the shapes out with a jig saw and sand until fair. If the keel sections are constant to the bottom and of the same chord length, it may only be necessary to make a couple. Identify the high spots with the template and remove them with either a large angle grinder or electric plane. (It is best not to tell the hire shop what you are planning to use it on!) The electric plane will remove lead if you are forced to go deeper than the surface filler, but will not remove iron. For this reason it is easier to rebuild the low side with filler, rather than trying to cut down an iron keel.

One clever trick to save time on a straight keel is to create an accurate raised profile at the top and bottom of the foil to act as a guide to screed the filler on. The principle is just the same as a plasterer nailing a temporary batten along a window opening to run his float along. After grinding the keel down to below minimum depth, wax the shaped edge of the template to act as a release agent, and apply a thick layer of car body filler to it. Hold it tightly against the relevant waterline section, and after five minutes it will have gone off sufficiently to remove the template, leaving a perfect male mould of the template section bonded on to the keel. Once you have such a raised profile at the top and bottom of the keel, use a sharp straight edge between the two ridges to screed on the filler to the correct profile.

Fill and fair any lows as described for the hull, but this time you will need a shorter sanding board, around 1.5 metres long. A length of closed cell foam glued on to plywood or a 45 mm plastic water pipe make an ideal sanding board, with just enough flexibility to bend around the draft of the keel or rudder. If a drawing is available of the keel or rudder the templates can be made straight from that, but often the practical solution to an asymmetric foil is simply to try to make it as thin and as symmetrical as possible, rather than attempting to recreate the designer's original intentions.

Lead keels which have been damaged require more major surgery. I once had only a few hours to patch up the keel of a 38 footer for Cowes Week which had just come from the Round Ireland Race and looked to have taken the overland route! Lumps of lead the size of a thumb had been displaced from the leading edge of the keel and I ended up dressing it back with a hammer; hardly a smooth finish. If the lead is exposed and has been pitted and scratched from more than just the odd grounding, use an electric plane to remove the rough areas and re-fair from there.

As you fill and sand either of the foils, watch carefully to see that no concavities are created in the aft sections, which can cause vibration at speed. Finish the trailing edges off with flat face to avoid damage. If you find the rudder does vibrate at times, the pundits say that the trailing edge should be rounded off. This is not always the root cause of such vibration, however, which could also be created by poor alignment of the rudder with the keel.

Finishing touches

Finally, after all your hard work on the bottom of the boat, it is time to protect it with a top coat and some form of antifouling. Race boats which are dry-sailed or spend most of their life sitting on a trailer are sometimes just left with a gel-coat or epoxy finish. But in the summer slime can quickly build up, even during a week's regatta, so it is worth considering some form of antifouling protection.

Most racing yachts use a hard racing antifouling, some brands of which now include Teflon. After all the hours of fairing it makes a nonsense of it to then apply a thick antifouling which will recreate unevenness and will need further sanding. The benefits of a Teflon based paint system is that it can have a film thickness of as little as 5 microns, compared with 100 microns for the conventional cruiser type antifouling. The smooth texture of the Teflon cuts the resistance between the hull and the water and so reduces drag. It also means that marine growth finds it harder to hang on. In practice a good wash and scrub between regattas is all that should be needed with this type of 'hard' antifouling, and a re-coat if necessary at the end of the year.

Whilst working on the underwater surfaces, don't forget to fair in any obtrusive skin fittings or replace them with flush fitting ones. Also make sure the rudder fits tight up under the hull, to prevent any upward flow and pressure loss between the two.

Improving rig controls and deck gear

If the boat is new to you, the best advice is to sail it for a while just as it is set up, even though some items of deckgear may patently be in the wrong place or not work effectively. As someone who gets to sail a wide variety of boats, you tend to become conditioned to liking things to hand as they were on the last boat you spent time on. As a result it is easy to shut your eyes to genuine improvements or better placement of equipment just because it is not what you are used to. Another important point is to try every piece of gear in a variety of wind strengths. Often there is a reason for a particular fitting which only becomes evident at 25 knots. As an example, the mainsheet trimmer on a cruiser racer I sailed with complained that the angle of the traveller cleat was too low and required him to push the rope into the cleat with his foot ever time. The cleat was duly angled up and worked a treat. However, the next weekend in 30 knots of breeze, we kept wiping out upwind because the mainsheet could not be dumped quickly enough. With the boat heeled and the mainsheet trimmer sitting out, the lead angle had changed, requiring the traveller line to be lifted up almost vertically before it would release the traveller car.

So, if you do change or move part of the deckgear always go sailing with it *before* the race. It is amazing how one small change of equipment affects the ergonomics of everything else around it.

Running rigging

There have been major developments in the field of rope manufacture in the last five years with High Modulus Polyethylene rope (HMPE), gradually taking over from the Aramid fibres and polyester. HMPE is sold under the two brand names of Dyneema, manufactured in Holland, or Spectra, produced in the USA, whereas Aramid rope is always known as Kevlar. Kevlar was seen as a great improvement on Polyester and Nylon rope as

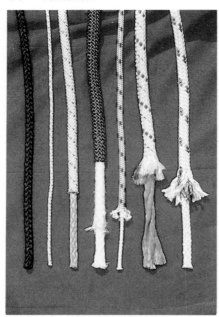

The options for running rigging.
Photo: *Martin Bean*

(left to right) 1. Plaited polypropylene rope
2. Plaited pre-stretched polyester
3. Vectran core, polyester cover
4. Spectra/Dyneema core, matt polypropylene inner jacket to help core grip cover. Cover polyester for abrasion resistenace and colour coding.
5. Lightweight sheet, bulky polypropylene cover, Spectra/Dyneema core for strength and low stretch.
6. Aramid core, polyester cover.
7. Double-braid, polyester core, polyester cover.

it is very strong and low stretch, but it was found that its flex-fatigue (resistance to repeated bending) was poor due to internal abrasion within the fibres, causing unpredictable failure. HMPE rope, in contrast, has very good flex-fatigue, is incredibly strong, nearly as low stretch as Kevlar, has excellent abrasion resistance, and is resistant to UV deterioration. The HMPE core is soft and silky to the touch and much easier and flexible to handle than Kevlar, which used to cut my hands to pieces on spinnaker legs. As a result of these properties, HMPE provides the best strength to weight ratio, which has important implications for saving weight aloft. In practice, a Spectra or Dyneema rope replacing a Polyester one can be 2 mm less in diameter for the same if not greater strength and less stretch.

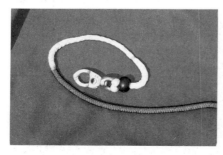

Typical halyard arrangement. The Spectra/Dyneema core of the rope is spliced to a snap shackle. The polyester cover is removed where the halyard would normally be in the mast. The polyester cover is retained at the cockpit end of the rope to ease handling.
Photo: *Martin Bean*

Because of the excellent abrasion resistance and flex-fatigue of HMPE fibres, the purpose of the Polyester cover is purely to ease handling and provide grip around winches and inside clutches and contributes little to strength. As a result, many riggers remove the outer cover from Spectra and Dyneema halyards, down to where they exit the mast to save even more weight. Sheets too benefit from being in HMPE rope, due to the low stretch (both recoverable and non-recoverable), good flex-fatigue and low comparative weight.

A knock-on effect from using relatively smaller diameter lines is the similar reduction in sizes of blocks and sheaves throughout the boat with obvious weight saving advantages for the rig too. Multi-purchase control lines can often be reduced to 4 mm, with consequent savings in weight and cost of the numerous blocks in the system. Handling then becomes the limiting factor in reducing the line size with HMPE rope. If you do not enjoy blistered hands, either buy a good pair of gloves or fit plastic balls to the end of the control lines or even trapeze handles. However, be sure when throwing away an old wire halyard with a 10 or 12 mm Polyester tail to replace it with an 8 mm HMPE rope. Many makes of rope clutch are very sensitive to line size, as they were designed to grip the old 10 or 12 mm standard diameters. In all cases the jaws of a clutch have to move relatively further before they will grip an 8 mm rope, which is when the annoying 'run-out' slippage occurs when you are trying to tension the genoa halyard. The little known cure is simply to add an extra length of Polyester cover to the area of the rope which passes through the clutch,

The vectran core is on the right, the polyester cover on the left.

Spectra/Dyneema core, with polypropylene inner jacket to help core and cover grip. The polyester outer cover aids colour coding and helps the rope grip in clutches and around winches.
Photos: *Martin Bean*

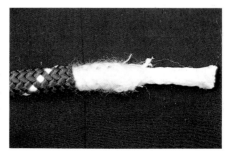

locally increasing the diameter and protecting the rope from wear by the clutch. This cover can be replaced when worn, or the whole halyard end-for-ended to increase its competitive lifespan.

The latest 'hi-tech' rope is produced from the same liquid crystal polymers that first appeared in the black sails of the 1992 America's Cup, and is sold as Vectran. It is the ultimate low stretch fibre and does not have the long-term creep problem that HMPE exhibits under prolonged high loads.

Rig controls

The three most crucial sail controls that must always work quickly and efficiently are:

- Mainsheet system
- Kicker or vang
- Headsail sheeting system

Mainsheet systems

The mainsheet must be capable of very fine adjustment on the one hand and must also be able to be dumped in a hurry. For the type of racing boats that we are concerned with the choice is mainly between a block and tackle type arrangement or a layout originally favoured by the German Admiral's Cup Team. Here the sheet runs forward along the boom right to the goose-neck, down to the deck and then back to a pair of winches either side of the cockpit (Fig 2.4). The latter system was originally used on the old IOR 50 footers and 2 tonners, as the winches were placed halfway back in the cockpit in order to keep the weight of the winch and trimmer out of the back of the boat. However, designers now seem to have universally agreed on the benefits of the so-called German AC system, and it is increasingly

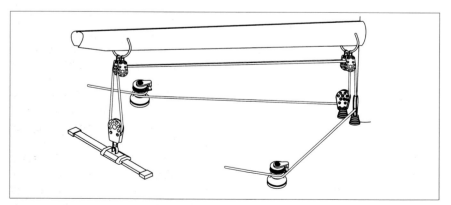

Fig 2.4 *The German Admiral's Cup mainsheet system.* Diagram: *Harken*

Here the twin tracks are fitted to allow a different sheeting angle for flat water and waves; the one car is moved from track to track as required.

means that the sheet comes straight from the lead block and on to the winch drum, cutting out the need for a friction inducing turning block. The benefit is quicker tacking and means that the trimmer, whilst winding in, is placed exactly in line with the genoa and can quickly gauge the leech position. But if the primaries are set well inboard then you are stuck with using a turning block. Check the foot block is positioned correctly, with the sheet in contact with as little of the sheave as possible in order to reduce friction to a minimum.

Other sail controls

With a little imagination most of the remaining sail controls can be rerouted to positions where they can either be reached from the rail or the pit. Leech lines which are led down the luff can be easily hooked up to a 2:1 tackle in a similar way to the cunningham. Think about when in a race each control is used and by whom, before deciding where to position it. The cunningham, for instance, goes on at the bottom mark and off at the windward mark, when the pit man is in position in the middle of the boat. In between hoisting halyards he or she can easily pull on the cunningham, so it makes sense to have the jammer located centrally on the coachroof. Similarly, reef lines should be led back to the pit from where the winches can be operated more easily. Small reefing winches set on the mast under the gooseneck are notoriously difficult to get at and are best removed. Their place should be taken by a set of two or three mast

Halyards, cunningham, outhaul, kicker, leech line, reef lines and topping lift are all led back to the pit on this IOR half tonner.

mounted instruments, showing boatspeed, true/apparent wind speed and true wind angle, so that all the crew can focus on achieving target speeds, whilst not having to look away far from the job they were doing.

The spinnaker pole downhaul or fore guy needs to be adjusted every time the guy is moved, so it makes sense to double end the fore guy and lead it back to a cleat next to the primary winch. There, the trimmer manning the guy can easily operate the fore guy too, which avoids having another crew member *not* sitting with legs out on a windy reach. The simplest way to convert the fore guy to a double ended system is to attach a double block to the pad eye on the fore deck and then lead the rope through a block shackled to the toe rail and then straight back along the deck to a jamming cleat close to the primary winch.

Buying new sails

Sails, unfortunately, are a consumable commodity with a limited competitive lifespan and should not be viewed as part of the capital cost of the boat. Obviously budget has much to do with the number and frequency with which sails are replaced, but let's take an example of a typical 38ft cruiser racer on a limited budget. What factors should the owner consider when buying new sails?

Firstly, identify the most worn out sails in the inventory and work out an order of priority for which ones should be replaced first. If you get in the habit of taking photos of the fore and aft sails when each is new and then every few months, you will be able to keep track of how their shape is changing. Expect old genoas to go draft aft (the designed maximum depth position slips back as the fabric breaks down), round in the back and possibly hooked in the last 40 mm of the leech. Tired mainsails also go draft aft but the main indication is a stretched, open leech. Often the mid leech will stretch permanently before the top section, which makes it hard to get the twist right. (See chapter 4 for how to measure depth and draft from a photograph.) Some sailmakers will even assess your sail shots for you and provide a report on the shape and state of each sail (with their recommendations for replacements, of course!).

You will probably have a good idea as to where the weak link in the sail inventory lies. Racing an IMX 38 in a Spring Series a few years back against a number of sister ships, we enjoyed good pace under No 1 genoa conditions but often struggled against one particular IMX which had a high modulus, Aramid No 3. (High modulus sail fabrics include such brand names as Kevlar, Technora, Spectra, Dyneema and Vectran.) Our own boat had a Mylar No 3 which was slightly smaller in LP (luff perpendicular), and combined with the greater stretch of Mylar resulted in a less powerful sail. However, racing under the Channel Handicap System, we enjoyed a small 0.002 TCF rating advantage over the rival IMX 38 as a result of not carrying any so called 'hi-tech' sails. So the question was, if we bought a Kevlar No 3 would the boat be able to sail to the increased rating? Clearly the other IMX 38 that beat us in the Spring Series did so, but that was a breezy series when jibs were used in over 75 percent of the races. Considering the rest of the sail inventory, I knew we had a gap of around 17–20 knots. The heavy No 1 could at a push be carried up to 20 knots, but was only fast up to 18 knots. We then changed to the No 3 which only became quick above 20 knots (all apparent wind speeds). Going upwind in the 17–22 knots band thus created a tricky headsail choice. Ordering a 135 percent No 2 was one option, but such a sail would have too specialised a wind range, and would involve extra headsail changes which are to be avoided in close inshore racing. What the boat needed was a big, powerful Kevlar No 3 with the maximum 98 percent LP, which would only just sheet on to the track. This would provide the necessary margin of overlap in range with the heavy No 1. Shapewise, I prefer a 'knuckle fronted' sail – a straight backed sail which can be set deep and powerful at the bottom of its wind range. Being built from Kevlar, it should not stretch and get deeper when the breeze increases and you need to flatten the jib off and blade out the top. On the other hand, why add an extra 0.002 to the TCF (Time Correction Factor), when in every race below 18 knots the sail would never come out of the bag?

The decision was made to order the new No 3 before the half-used Mylar sail became uncompetitive, so that the option was available of entering a likely light airs regatta with the old Mylar sail and saving the 0.002 points on the rating or racing with the Kevlar jib at windy venues. CHS sailing instructions usually require the yacht's rating to be confirmed a week or so before the first race, and do not permit reductions in TCF during a series – there is always a gamble in playing the rating game.

Choosing the most suitable fabrics

Under the old IOR, International Measurement System and US PHRF system there is no rating penalty for high modulus sail fabrics, which takes the rating element out of the equation. Boats with flexible racing spars are the best equipped to get the increased performance out of a high modulus fabric mainsail as the mast has to be sensitively adjusted to get the best from the sail. A Dacron or Mylar mainsail is better suited to cruiser racers under 35 foot which typically carry a less 'tweakable' stick. Mainsails of this size and smaller in Dacron and Mylar are not subject to loads sufficient to cause major distortion, so long as a suitable fabric weight is used. The inherent stretch in these materials can be used to advantage to produce a sail which can be made to change shape significantly as the conditions dictate through use of the sail controls. From around 38 feet up, the benefits stack up in favour of the high modulus fabrics. A comparable Dacron sail for a 40 footer would be very heavy, the degree of uncontrollable distortion would make it uncompetitive racing against a Kevlar or Spectra sail, without any allowance in rating.

When such fabrics first became available to sailmakers, we used to say that Kevlar produced much more of a fixed shape sail which could only accommodate a small range of mast-bend, whereas a Dacron mainsail was more readily adjustable to a wider wind range. Today the reality is the opposite, with the development of specialist 'front-end' materials which provide a degree of controllable bias stretch at the luff.

Several years ago when the CHS rule penalised all laminate fabrics there was a rating advantage for using a Dacron mainsail. A sailmaker who built the sails for a 40 foot Sigma 400 cruiser racer told me he had to design the mainsail to be flat in 0–12 knots so that once it began to stretch fuller above that it would stretch into the optimum depth for the wind strength and not become too full and uncontrollable. In other words, the sail had to be designed for a specific wind range. If you wanted a Dacron mainsail to be fast in light airs it would be hard to stop it stretching too deep and draft aft in a medium and heavy breeze. These days Mylar mainsails have become quite popular for CHS racing and represent a good halfway house between Dacron and Kevlar. They hold their shape better than Dacron, are lighter, but do still stretch – and permanently so when overloaded.

Some sailmakers still have doubts as to the lifespan of Mylar mains, but improved Mylar laminates are being developed all the time. The choice between the high modulus materials comes down to the Aramid fabrics such as Kevlar and Technora being used where minimal distortion is the prime factor, as is the case with most inshore and Grand Prix race boats.

HMPE fabrics (Dyneema and Spectra) get the nod in applications where flex-fatigue and durability are just as important as low stretch and weight saving, and are commonly seen on long distance race boats and big cruising yachts.

It can be harder to spot exactly when a spinnaker becomes old and slow, but telltale signs to look out for are hooky luffs and distortion in the head. This distortion means that the sail becomes deeper as bulges appear in the head, and results in a loss of projected area. The best place to assess its shape is from off the boat, looking at the sail from side on.

It is a false economy to try to get away with only two kites, a 0.5 oz and a 0.75 oz, even if the 1.5 oz never seems to be used. The quickest way to blow a 0.75 oz is on a close reach in 25 knots plus. With the wide variety in race courses these days, most race boats increasingly opt for an all-purpose shape 0.5 oz and 0.75 oz kite and a 1.5 oz reacher. There is little

The lighter, more stretchy front-end material is clearly evident in the white panels on the sails of this IMS 40 footer.

In a typical handicap fleet, some boats will opt for Mylar sails (eg K4243T) while race boats will tend to choose high modulus fabrics (Kevlar, Spectra or Dyneema) to reduce stretch further.

room for specialised spinnakers (including asymmetric reachers) when limited to three sails. However, crews with good boat handling racing inshore tend to use the 0.75 oz AP sail downwind in most conditions when spinnakers are flown, and keep it in one piece. The 1.5 oz can therefore become a flat reaching sail and the reserve 'chicken chute'. Crews prone to wild broaches and crash gybes would be better advised to use more of an all-purpose 1.5 oz kite and put it up every time the wind is over 20 knots, whatever the wind angle.

There is insufficient room here to look at sails in any detail, so this basic advice will have to suffice. Make sure your chosen sailmaker knows what sort of racing you have planned, how long you expect the sails to last, and the exact rig dimensions for your boat.

A final point to be aware of is that as we drive our boats harder and faster, the loadings on various fittings may at times be considerably more than the designer originally calculated. Upgrading to laminate sails, changing to HMPE running rigging or even just racing with extra crew will create higher loads on key equipment. If in doubt as to which size block you need for a certain application, consult the hardware manufacturer's catalogue, which should list safe working loads and breaking strengths for each item.

3. Tuning the Rig

Setting up the rig correctly is possibly the most neglected element of yacht racing. The reasons owners give for sailing around with badly sorted rigs range from 'It takes too long to fiddle around with it', 'It's how the yard put it in', to 'It's always been like this.' In reality owners can be put off adjusting their rigs either because they don't know what set up they should be trying to achieve, or that changing it might make the boat go slower. However, without the mast set up properly you might as well not bother going racing, so fundamental is it to performance. Even the fastest sails in the world will be slow or lack pointing if the rig they are hung up on is falling away to leeward or over bending fore-and-aft.

During my time as a sailmaker I would occasionally be asked by a customer to go and look at a sail which was not performing. Often the complaint would be that the boat would not point or that the mainsail lacked power. Invariably those telltale symptoms led to the discovery of a problem within the set up of the rig rather than a fault within the sail.

In order to examine the way in which different rigs should be set up it is important to know precisely what we mean when we describe various terms you will come across:

- Mast bend
- Pre-bend
- Rake
- Spreader deflection

Mast bend is taken here to mean a variable amount of fore-and-aft bend, depending on how hard the backstay or runners are pulled on and how tightly the mainsail is sheeted. Its use is to control and vary mainsail shape across the wind range

Pre-bend refers to a different type of bend. It is still in the fore-and-aft plane and is the amount of permanent bend set into the rig via shroud tension, shroud position and spreader angle, that you would see in the mast at the dock with no sails up and no runner or backstay tension. The reason for pre-bending the mast is predominantly to take fullness out of the sail and to match it to the curve of the luff cut into the mainsail.

Aft rake is the degree to which the top of the mast is angled back towards the stern. If a mast is plumb upright it is said to have no rake and if it leans forward it is not surprisingly known as forward rake. The amount of rake is determined by headstay length. Apart from being fast upwind, aft rake affects the amount of helm felt on the tiller. As the mast is raked progressively aft so in turn the centre of effort of the sail plan is moved. If the centre of effort is positioned aft of the centre of resistance of the hull and foils, the boat will tend to head up into the wind; a phenomenon known as windward helm (Fig 3.1).

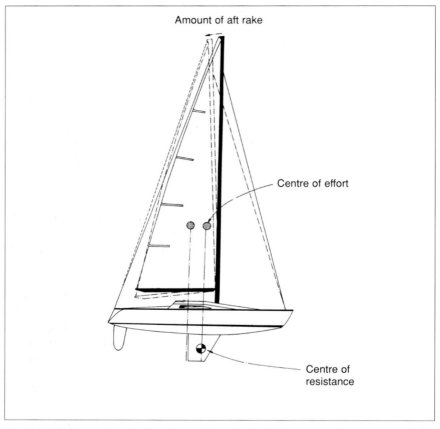

Fig 3.1 *If the centre of effort is positioned aft of the centre of resistance of the hull and foils, the boat will tend to head up into the wind, a phenomenon known as windward helm.*

It is important to have a method of measuring the amount of rake your boat carries, so it can be reproduced again, or used to compare settings with other fast yachts. Small boats and dinghies commonly use a tape measure hoisted to the mast head and measured to a datum point on the transom. This method is not so easy to use on a tall rig, where the windage on the tape measure can pull the tape out of your hands, even if it were

Sighting up the mast on the dock will give you some idea if the rig tension is pulling the mast over in one direction. In this case the starboard cap shroud needs to be eased and/or the port one tightened.

long enough. Instead, hang a steadying weight off the end of the main halyard, such as a winch handle or a bucket of water; and with the boom horizontal, mark the position at which the halyard touches the boom. Measure along to the back of the mast from the mark to find the amount of rake.

Spreader deflection. The way to understand the action of the spreader is to consider the outboard end to be anchored firmly by the shroud and that it is the mast end of the spreader which can move, resulting in the mast being pushed forward or aft, depending upon the degree of sweep or deflection of the spreader. The degree of deflection can most easily be measured by placing a straight edge against the spreader tips and measuring from the middle of the straight edge to the aft face of the mast. Increasing the deflection will increase pre-bend and vice versa.

Tuning principles – getting your eye in

At first sight, tuning the rig can be a complex and off-putting issue, especially if you have a complicated multi-spreader or swept back rig. The answer is to break down the problem by dividing mast bend into two distinct divisions: sideways bend and fore-and-aft bend.

Sideways bend

The only way to see if your mast is straight sideways is to sight up it whilst sailing close hauled. Sighting the mast at the dock will give you some idea as to whether the rig tension is pulling the mast over in one direction, but if the rig is slack and the mast falls off to leeward, it will not be evident until you go sailing.

I tend to look up the front of the mast first, assuming that the base of the mast comes out of the deck straight and then try to produce the lines of the mast vertically upwards in my mind's eye, and see if the mast actually follows the 'produced' bottom section. Some sections have a machined groove running down the front which can act as a handy sight line and is easier to sight than the two tapering sides of the mast. However, race boat rigs often carry considerable fore-and-aft bend upwind and with the main sheeted in hard, the top section may not be visible when sighting from in front, as it is peeled back from view. In this case, I slide under the boom and sight up the luff groove from under the gooseneck. Again, eyeball a vertical line up from the luff groove at the base of the mast and see if it matches up with the actual luff groove or mainsail track. Occasionally you may come across a mast with a twisted luff groove, in which case either sight from the front of the mast or use the side walls as a guide.

The top, unsupported section of a fractional rig will always fall away to leeward in a breeze, so do not worry too much about tip fall off. It is from where the uppers intersect the mast downwards that should be straight. When racing in heavy air it pays with some fractional rigged boats to de-power the rig by encouraging the top mast to bend to leeward, but in terms

Sighting up the front of the mast to check that it is straight sideways. Pulling on the lower will have the effect of tightening the shroud and can help you decide if the lower needs to be tensioned.

of setting the boat up in the first instance for average conditions and maximum VMG (velocity made good) we need to set the mast straight sideways.

Fore-and-aft bend

Fore-and-aft bend is completely different from lateral bend and is mainly controlled by a different set of rigging. We have already seen that keeping the mast straight sideways is vital to holding up the mainsail leech and to provide the vital pointing ability. Fore-and-aft bend, on the other hand, is more about controlling depth in the mainsail and hence is basically a power up/power down control.

The mainsail luff curve should be cut to fit the mast bend, but slight mismatches can be allowed for by localised straightening or bending of the relevant portion of the mast. Fore-and-aft bend is controlled by the relative position of the mast heel and deck chocks, runners, checkstays, backstay and mainsheet tension.

Common principles of mast tune

Having looked at the different aspects of mast bend, how should the rig ideally be set up? It is hard to generalise as there are so many different combinations of rigs popular these days on race boats, racer cruiser and cruiser racers.

In principle the mast should be set dead straight sideways and have enough rig tension to keep it straight. Many one-design keelboats, such as the International Dragon, J-24 and even offshore one-design classes, will fine tune the rig tension to match the expected wind strength in an

---

Table 3.1 *J-24 Rig Tension Guide*

These are the rig tensions which have been found to produce the correct forestay tension for each wind band and a mast bend of 50–65 mm. Shroud tensions are measured using a Loos Tension Gauge, Model B on 4.7 mm (3/16ths) stainless steel wire and are quoted in kgs and lbs.

	True wind strength in knots		
	0–8	9–16	17+
Upper shroud tension (lbs/kgs)	550/*249*	750/*340*	950/*430*
Lower shroud tension	300/*136*	750/*340*	1050/*476*

Note how the lower shrouds are progressively tightened up more than the upper shrouds as the wind increases, to promote sideways bend.

Table 3.2 *International Dragon Rig Tension Guide*

Shroud tensions are measured on 5 mm Dyform wire and the values come straight from the scale on a Loos Tension Gauge, Model B.

	True wind strength in knots		
	0–8	**9–17**	**18+**
Upper shroud tension (scale reading)	26	35	40
Lower shroud tension	8	20	30

attempt to keep the mast dead straight in maximum power conditions, and then encourage it to bend to leeward when it becomes faster to de-power to avoid excessive helm. Tables 3.1 and 3.2 provide examples of this with specific rig tensions for the J-24 and International Dragon. In practice, multi-spreader race boat rigs are too complicated to adjust for every condition, and once set up straight are left so throughout the series or regatta. They should, of course, be checked before each race.

Consider the simplest possible set up of a mast with a pair of upper shrouds, a single set of spreaders and a pair of lowers. If the shroud base is in line with the mast then the shrouds are purely supporting the mast sideways, which simplifies the understanding considerably. Figs 3.2 and 3.3 show the effects of varying rig tensions.

The important point to notice here is that the actual amount of rig tension in the uppers and lower is not always the critical factor; rather it is the relative difference between the two. The reason for the situation shown in Fig 3.2 could either be due to:

- the lowers being too loose, requiring the middle of the mast to be pulled up to windward so as to be 'in column' with the rest of the spar.
- the cap shrouds being too tight, causing the spreader to push the mast to leeward. You can imagine that as the spreader deflects the line of the shroud, the more tension that is applied to it, the more it will try to take up a straight line. As it does so it forces the spreader sideways, so pushing the middle of the mast to leeward. The leeward shroud, by virtue of being on the unloaded, leeward side, is relatively slack and so produces less sideways thrust on the spreader and so the mast pops to leeward.

Fig 3.3 shows what happens if the lowers are too tight in comparison to the uppers. Again the problem could be cured by:

- easing the lowers until the mast becomes in-column.
- tightening the cap shrouds until the mast is straight.

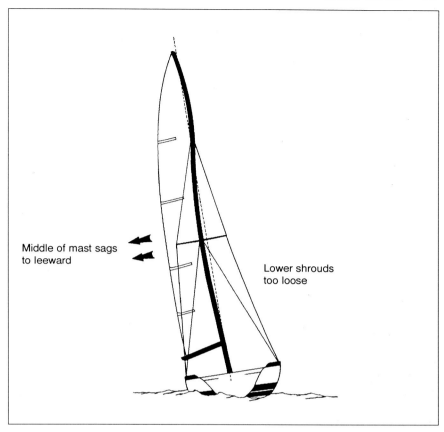

Fig 3.2 *With the lowers too loose the mast falls away to leeward at the spreaders, effectively hooking the top mast up to windward. This creates a mainsail too full in the middle with a closed top leech, unfair twist, and results in a lack of pointing and an uncontrollable sail.*

So which option do you choose in each of the above cases? It is true that the upper shrouds need to be tight enough to keep the mast straight in everything up to overpowered conditions. However, more rig tension than is necessary for a given wind speed is slow because all it does is add extra compression to the mast and creates a less responsive rig.

Tuning the upper shrouds

The first step is to find an 'average', mid-range setting for the upper shroud tension. Before you do anything else you need to check that the mast is dead centre in the boat. If the rig is out of the boat, run a fine line or cotton down the centreline and measure carefully that the mast hole is

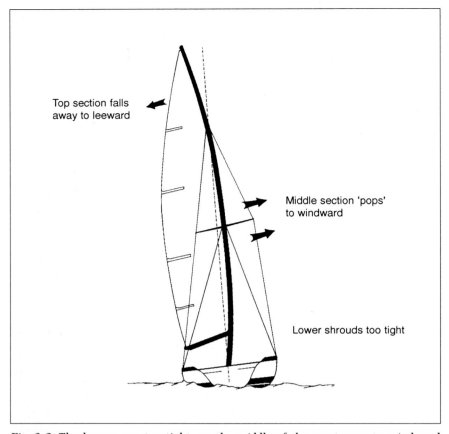

Fig 3.3 *The lowers are too tight, so the middle of the mast pops to windward whilst the top falls off to leeward.*

exactly in the middle. If not, pack one side with a nylon or formica shim so that the mast block is dead central and chocked solid. With the mast in situ, the best you can do is to measure from each side of the mast to a similar station on the gunwale, although this is not as accurate – hulls are not always as symmetrical as you would expect.

Next, with boat at the dock and in calm conditions, make fast the main halyard at a point which, when pulled hard, just touches the toe rail at a station in line with the mast. Repeat the operation at the same position on the other side of the boat. When the halyard lengths are the same the mast is straight. Now tension up the rig by winding up the bottle screws a couple of turns at a time and then take up a similar amount on the other side. Count the number of turns or use a rig tension meter to ensure you keep matching tensions on both shrouds. The reason for alternating sides whilst winding up the tension on the upper shrouds is that the mast may exhibit 'memory' as the rig becomes tight. If the shrouds were completely slack and the port side was wound up to a high tension before taking up on the starboard side, the mast would clearly lean to port. However, even after the same tension had been applied to the starboard shroud you might find that the mast still bent to port slightly. Once tacking upwind, the loading would tend to straighten the mast out, but it is best to achieve as straight a mast as possible (sideways) at the dock before you go sailing.

How tight should the upper or cap shrouds be in initially? Well, sufficient so that in 15 knots maximum power conditions, when the boat will be heeled at around 20–22°, the mast is held dead straight. If the top mast where the shrouds are connected is falling off on both tacks, then the cap shrouds are probably too loose, but check first that the problem is not caused by overtight lowers or too short spreaders.

It is well worth getting into the habit of checking the mast before every start:

- to ensure the lowers are correctly set for the expected wind speed.
- to check the upper shrouds have not lost tension due to stretch or new fittings bedding in after a heavy airs race.

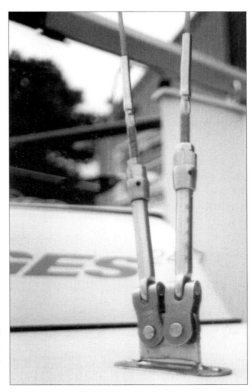

Calibrated turnbuckles (visible just above the toggle) are an easy way of repeating rig settings accurately.

Take the lowers up hand tight equally both sides and then sail upwind, sighting up the mast as before. Once you are happy that the top and bottom are basically in line (ignoring for the moment any bending in the middle of the mast) and that the leeward upper is still in tension at 22° of heel, then you have found your medium upper shroud setting. Record this tension either by marking the bottlescrews, counting the threads showing each side, or by using a suitable tension meter.

Tuning the lowers

Now look at the middle of the mast whilst still beating and decide if the mast is falling in or not at spreader height. If you are not sure if the mast is exactly straight, the technique I use is to pull on the windward lower

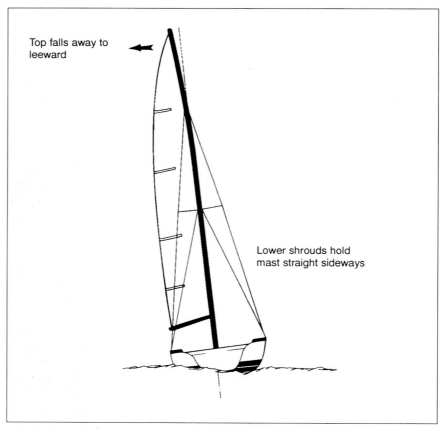

Fig 3.4 *The correct lower shroud setting for medium airs. The middle of the mast is held straight and the mast is in column all the way to the upper shrouds. There is a slight amount of top fall-off from the unsupported top section.*

whilst sighting the middle of the mast and see the difference it makes. If pulling on the lower makes the mid mast 'pop' to windward, then the tension is about right; but if it does not, then another turn on the rigging screw is required. By pulling on the lower and so bending the mast, it somehow makes it easier to see if the mast is in line. It is just a matter of 'getting your eye in', but it can be quite hard at first when staring up the mast to see when the middle of the mast is straight and when the unsupported top of the mast is bending off to leeward.

You will find that the lowers need relatively fewer turns than the uppers. Each turn puts more tension into the lower shrouds than would a single turn on the uppers, due to the shorter length of the lowers and the lesser loading they experience. For this reason it is very easy to over tension the lowers, so beware. The perfect lower shroud setting for medium conditions is to pull the middle of the mast just up to windward, to bring the whole mast into line athwartships (Fig 3.4).

In heavy airs one-design boats which do not have a wide range of headsails with which to depower, such as the Dragon, Soling and Star, do so by allowing the top half of the mast to fall off to leeward. This allows the mainsail leech to twist off more easily. The top half of the rig is encouraged to bend to leeward by tightening up the lowers so that they become relatively tighter than the uppers. The mast is held straight up to the

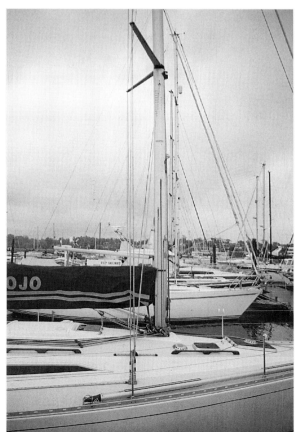

The fractional, swept back rig.

spreaders and thereafter starts to bend off in a fair curve, helping to open up almost half of the mainsail leech.

Having looked at the general principles of how the rig should be set up, how exactly does it work on your own rig? Each of the four major rig types requires quite different tuning techniques to set them up and rules learnt from one rig do not always apply to others, due to the differing geometry of the rigging.

The fractional swept back rig

This rig has long been the favourite of cruiser racer designers, who draw in the shroud base angled back behind the mast, commonly at around 20°. The reason is to provide a measure of fore-and-aft support to the mast, even though runners may also be fitted to reduce headstay sag when racing. The thinking is that the club racer, who may also use his dual purpose craft for the occasional cruise with the family, will not want a rig that comes crashing down every time someone is a little late pulling on the runner after a tack or gybe.

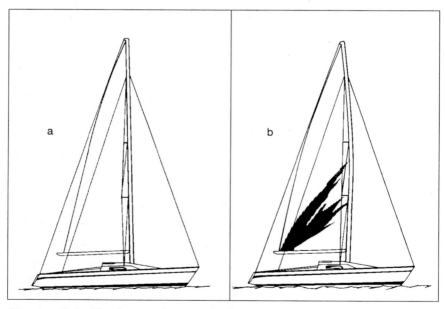

Diagram 3.5. The fractional swept back rig. (a) In 12–15 knot maximum power conditons the mast is held straight by tightening the lowers, pulling the mast into column and forcing depth into the mainsail. (b) In heavy airs, easing the lowers allows the middle of the mast to bend, so flattening the mainsail. Overbend creases begin to appear running from the clew to the luff.

Table 3.3 *Relative Rig Tensions for a Fractional Swept Back Rig (Sigma 38 one-design)*

Because there is no tension meter readily available for 10 mm stainless steel wire, the following table of rig tensions can only be relative. It is assumed the rig has been set up straight as described above, and the upper shrouds tensioned so that the leeward shroud does not go slack when the yacht is heeled over 15°. Lower shroud tension should give medium air pre-bend of 100–150 mm.

	True Wind Strength in Knots		
	0–8	**9–17**	**18+**
Upper and diagonal shrouds	Tight	Tight	Tight + 2 turns
Lower shrouds	Mean setting −2 turns	Mean setting	Mean setting −2 turns

This type of rig is by far the most common on European cruiser racers, which are the yachts many people start their racing in. Unfortunately it is also one of the more complex. Whereas previously we sought to simplify the workings of the rig by breaking it down to fore-and-aft and athwartships bend, the swept back rig has to be considered as a three-dimensional problem. The fact that the shroud plates are positioned some 20° aft of the mast means that although their primary role is to hold the mast up sideways, they also contribute to the fore-and-aft support. In the case of the uppers this means that the shroud tension also serves to keep the headstay tight, and in the absence of runners, is the main method of doing so. Once the uppers have been tensioned hard so that the mast is held straight, any further tension will simply serve to add compression to the spar, resulting in increased pre-bend. This pre-bend could be reduced by angling the spreader aft as you would with a dinghy rig, so that the middle of the mast is pulled back, but in reality yacht mast spreaders are not readily adjustable.

In practice, the middle of the mast is best straightened by tensioning the lowers, pulling the mid section aft, back into column. You would want a straight mast in 12–15 knot maximum power conditions, when keeping the lower mast straight deepens the mainsail and helps to keep the mast in column, so enhancing tension in the upper shrouds, which in turn keeps the headstay tight. It follows that, in contrast to the in-line rig, as the breeze builds and the boat is over-powered, it is necessary to ease the lowers in order for the mid mast to bend and so flatten the mainsail (Fig 3.5).

The fractional in-line rig (with runners)

The in-line rig is one of the simpler rigs to tune, as the rigging can be neatly divided into fore-and-aft and athwartship supports. This rig is generally found on pure race boats, where the demands of performance outweigh those of safety or ease of handling.

Compared with the swept back rig, the in-line arrangement permits:

- precise control of headstay sag via runner tension.
- the ability of the mast to be pulled forward downwind, raising the sail plan into higher wind speeds away from the surface boundary layer and removing the aft rake.
- the boat to run squarer downwind as the boom can be let out further before it hits the shrouds.
- the headstay to be sagged off in light airs by easing the runner or, if necessary in very light conditions, by pulling the mast forward with a spare halyard clipped on to the bow to power up the front of the genoa.
- the lowers can be adjusted for heavy airs to help promote top mast lean to leeward to de-power the main by reducing heel and helm and opening the mainsail leech, ie increasing the twist.

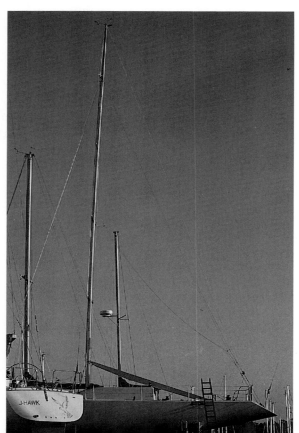

The fractional, swept back rig.

Sideways control

Race boat masts, in an effort to reduce the weight and associated pitching moment of the spar, are built from smaller and lighter sections than are found on dual purpose yachts. In order to hold up such flexible masts race boat rigs will usually have two or three sets of spreaders, supported by corresponding pairs of diagonal shrouds. These are best considered as a second and third set of lower shrouds as their role is to prevent the mast sagging to leeward at each spreader. As we discussed earlier, the only way to tune lower and diagonal shrouds is when sailing upwind in 14 knots or more, because in less wind the loading on the rig may not be sufficient to cause any sideways sag or bend.

If faced with a small section of the mast sagging to leeward, tension the lower or diagonal which attaches to the spar nearest to the centre of the kink. Again, check first that the problem is not caused by the cap shroud being too tight, pushing the spreader to leeward and pulling the top to windward, giving the appearance of the mast sagging to lee.

Whilst tuning the diagonals, check that the spreaders are fixed solid at the mast end and that the height of the outboard end is such that is bisects the angle of the shroud.

Fore-and-aft bend

The fore-and-aft bend of a fractional, in-line rig is controlled by runner tension, checkstays, the backstay and by chocking the mast at deck level.

The bottom section of the mast is usually very stiff, as it has to be strong enough to withstand the main boom and spinnaker pole thrust, and is locally reinforced by the spinnaker pole track. If there is a need to bend or straighten this lower section in order to fit the mainsail or to flatten an overfull sail, do so by adjusting the chocks in front of the mast. Add chocks in front of the spar to straighten it, or remove them and re-place them behind to permit more low down bend upwind. If there is no room to add chocks at deck level, the same effect can be gained by moving the heel of the mast forward to reduce pre-bend, and vice versa.

Working upwards, there is little that can be done to straighten the mast at the first spreader if the shroud base is in line with the mast. If the mainsail luff curve does not match the bend in this area, the answer is to have the sail altered rather than trying to make the mast bend to suit.

Bend in the middle of the mast is controlled by the checkstays, which are like a fine tune, straightening the mast to power up the mainsail in medium air. When and how much 'check' to use varies considerably between rigs and different depths of mainsails. The only way is to experiment and record fast settings. The important point to discover is what wind speed it pays to pull on the checkstay. It is much easier to recognise the signs when the boat is beginning to be over-powered and when the 'checks' need to be eased, as the front of the main will be lifting too much. In light to medium airs the checkstay will need to be brought on sooner in choppy conditions to provide power, than in flat water when you can hang on to a fine entried flat sail and benefit from the extra height generated.

The runners have little control over bend in the top third of the mast, as they pull directly against the forestay. However, they do add compression to the rig when winched up hard and so add to the bend below. Sailing a cruiser racer in a good breeze, the limiting factor on runner tension is usually the strength of the grinder – or how well the runner winch is attached to the deck! Race boats generally fit a load cell with a cockpit read-out to the forestay toggle to avoid over-straining the rig and in order to replicate fast settings readily.

The backstay on a fractional rig boat is a much under utilised sail shaping control. In recent years I have used it more and more in light airs to help sort out mainsails which are too deep or V shaped in the head for light conditions, and in order to twist open the upper leech. If this begins to tighten the headstay, which needs to be as loose as possible in such light conditions, tension up a spare halyard on to the bow fitting to keep tension off the headstay. As the backstay only affects the flexible tip section, there is no worry of it flattening off too much of the sail below the hounds.

How much you have to use the backstay in heavy air will depend on how inherently stiff the top, unsupported section is and whether diamond

The multi-spreader rig.

spreaders are fitted. The backstay is basically a tool to open the top main-sail leech, by simply shortening the distance from the tip of the mast to the transom. As the breeze builds and the mainsheet is graunched in tight in order to blade out flat the top of the main, the last few inches of the leech can become too closed. The backstay should then be used to return the leech to its previous open attitude, easing pressure on the helm.

Multi-spreader rigs

Multi-spreader rigs are limited to Grand Prix race boats where the weight and windage of the rig has been reduced to a minimum. As a consequence, the mast requires a greater degree of support, so extra sets of spreaders are employed to hold the flexible spar in column sideways.

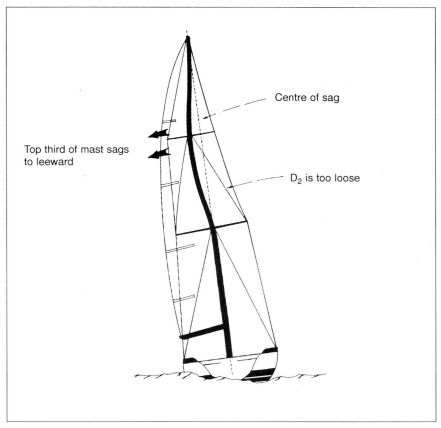

Fig 3.6 *Multi-spreader rig. The problem with a two or three spreader rig is pin-pointing exactly which diagonal shroud is too slack. It will be the diagonal at the centre of the sagging panel that will need tensioning.*

The problem with a two or three spreader rig is to pinpoint exactly which diagonal is tight or too loose; but with an inherently flexible spar the section each shroud supports is relatively small and it will be the diagonal at the centre of the sagging panel that will need tensioning (Fig 3.6).

Invariably the greater the number of diagonals, the more opportunities there are to get things wrong. If you notice one spreader sagging to leeward, first check that the problem is not caused by the upper being overtight, then tack the boat and take up a couple of turns on the relevant diagonal whilst it is to lee and unloaded. Never try to tension rigging screws when under high load as the threads can be damaged. It is much easier just to tack the boat and then tack back to assess the alteration. In the case of discontinuous rod rigging it may not be practical to adjust the diagonal rods which may be linked at the spreader tip whilst underway; they will have to be altered at the dock.

In practice, multi-spreader rigs all use some form of rod rigging, and the rig tension is usually applied by jacking up the heel of the mast with a hydraulic jack and then packing the heel up with aluminium shims.

Achieving a dead straight mast is a little like tuning a piano, with so many separate rods to tension correctly. The job can be very confusing as it can be hard to identify which rod is responsible for a kink in the mast. It is often a matter of trial and error, although an experienced eye will take much less time to sort it. Once the sideways set-up is right it tends not to be touched for fear of upsetting the tune. As the fore-and-aft bend can be adjusted completely independently, there is no real need to adjust the athwartships set-up for different conditions. Reducing the rig tension slightly for light airs may reduce the compression on the spar, but it will slacken off the diagonals relatively more than the cap shrouds and easily reintroduce sag into the mast. The best way to halve the compression in the area where it does most harm – the flexible top mast – is to fit a masthead halyard lock.

As far as fore-and aft bend is concerned the picture is the same as for the fractional in-line rig, since the fore-and-aft rigging components are identical.

The masthead rig

Tuning the masthead rig demands a whole new set of priorities, compared with the methods we have looked at for fractional rigs. The more racy masthead boats, such as the IMX 38, carry in-line spreaders and shrouds much like fractional yachts – some with lightweight runners which act as checkstays to limit and centre the fore-and-aft bend. Safety conscious production boats are likely to have the shrouds placed aft of the mast and may not carry runners or checks.

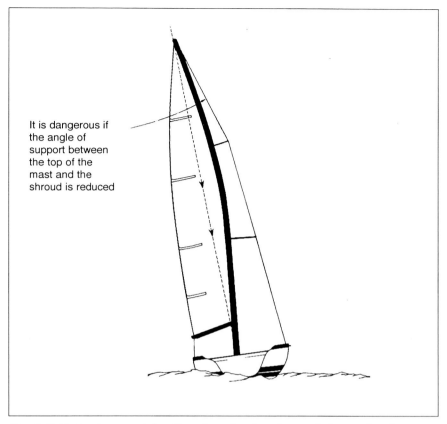

It is dangerous if the angle of support between the top of the mast and the shroud is reduced

Fig 3.7 *If the top mast is allowed to bend to leeward the angle of support becomes reduced further and will at some stage result in failure.*

On a masthead boat it is the backstay rather than the runners which is the major control of fore-and-aft bend, and like the runners on a fractional rig, serve to control the all important headstay tension.

Whilst sailors may think a masthead rig is safer in that you can gybe without having to worry about any runners, the lateral support issues can be more dangerous. The masthead rig must be kept straight sideways at all times. You cannot afford to try the fractional rig trick of winding up the lowers in the breeze and letting the top fall off, as the geometry of the upper shrouds gets a bit scary. As the cap shrouds are subject to the leverage of the entire length of the mast, the tension in the stay upwind can be considerable. As the top mast bends and the angle between the mast and the upper shroud becomes less, so further tension is required to hold the spar up. If the top mast is allowed to bend more to leeward, the angle of support becomes reduced further and will at some stage result in failure (Fig 3.7).

Another reason for keeping a masthead rig straight in heavy airs is that if the mast moves out of column, pulling on the backstay actually starts to loosen the headstay, as the top of the mast is being pulled to leeward as well as down. This means that in strong winds when you are trying to flatten out the headsail, it will become fuller and will lose pointing ability (Fig 3.8).

In heavy airs the uppers will stretch relatively more than the shorter diagonals, resulting in the top mast falling away because the D2 is now relatively too tight and promotes the top mast lean. To avoid this, set up the D2 slightly slacker so that the spreader will sag to leeward a little in light airs, but as the breeze gets up the tension in the D2 will be in sympathy with the stretching upper shroud. Remember what we said at the beginning of the chapter; that it is not the *absolute* rig tension that matters

Backstay tension pulls mast tip to leeward and down if mast is not held straight

Fig 3.8 *If a masthead rig is not held closely in column, applying backstay tension only serves to pull the tip of the mast to leeward and down, so bending the spar further out of column and slackening the fore stay.*

most, but the relative difference between the vertical upper shrouds and the diagonal and lower shrouds.

Reducing stretch in the standing rigging

In tandem with developments in new materials for ropes and sailcloth fabrics, there is now a wide spectrum of wire and rod rigging available as well as methods of reducing the all-up weight of the rigging. Beginning with conventional 1×19 stainless steel wire, a lower stretch version is available which is ideal for dinghies and keelboats with high rig tensions and class

Fig 3.9 *Dyform Ixia wire has a higher elastic modulus, due to the interlocking nature of the shrouds and so has a higher breaking load and greater resistance to stretch.* Diagram: *Norseman Gibb*

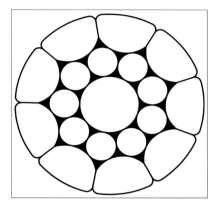

rules that prohibit rod Dyform wire is made with less inherent twist than the conventional 1×19 construction, and each strand is almost square in cross-section. It is these square edges bearing on each other which lock the strands together into a wire and make possible a straighter orientation of the strands.

The first thing that happens to a standard 1×19 wire shroud when subject to high load is that the twist in the wire begins to straighten out, so lengthening the wire, in the same way as crimp straightens out in woven sailcloth. The less twisted strands of Dyform wire reduce this distension, and when used in conjunction with a calibrated turnbuckle can make tuning the rig a much more accurate and repeatable process. Many keelboats such as the Etchells 22, J-24, Soling and Dragon, which alter rig tensions before each race, rely purely on the numbers etched on to the barrel of the turnbuckle. It is impossible to use a tension meter accurately when the boat is bobbing about on a mooring or when the sails are up.

As a continuation of the same line of development, the logical progression in low stretch rigging for yachts has to be a single straight rod. Standard rod rigging is known as nitronic rod, but for high load applications on Grand Prix boats where weight is an important consideration, cobalt rods are preferred. The ultimate in weight saving is titanium, carbon or Kevlar rods which are around 30 per cent lighter than nitronic rod, although their applications are limited. Top race boats have found Kevlar rods ideal for runners and checkstays and titanium backstays produce a considerable saving in both windage and weight.

If your pocket is not bottomless, a less expensive route to reducing the weight of your standing rigging it to opt for a discontinuous system. A single span of rod runs from the chainplates to the first spreader and then succeeding spans are linked from spreader tip to spreader tip with a progressive reduction in rod diameter and weight. Each section should have its own turnbuckle to allow independent adjustment of each span. The discontinuous nature of the system does make tuning the rig a little more complicated as you have to work out which span of the shrouds is too tight or loose in order to take a kink out of the mast. The fact that the terminal fittings can pivot in their end cups at each spreader tip reduces rod fatigue and should increase the competitive lifespan of the rig.

Obviously, failure of a single rod could be catastrophic and very expensive in these days when it is nigh-on impossible to insure 'hi-tech' race boat rigs. Rigs can be surveyed either visually or with a non-destructive rig tester which measures the electrical resistance of swaged wire terminals and can pick up on any hidden broken strands. This means the rig can be easily checked whilst it is still in the boat. Testing rod is not so easy but some riggers use a dye-penetrant test to look for cracks in the head of the rod. The only other way to inspect a suspect section is to have it X-rayed. No one is sure of the working lifespan of a rod rig, but insurance companies are becoming increasingly twitchy about 8–10 year old rigs and are demanding rig surveys. Race boat rigs that are sailed hard and often should certainly be surveyed every 2–3 years, apart from the visual check over, cleaning and greasing of all threads and terminals which should be part of the pre-season maintenance and prior to each major regatta.

4. Going Faster Upwind

Now that the boat has been thoroughly prepared and the rig carefully tuned, good upwind speed should not be hard to attain, given a reasonable suit of sails. The difference in boatspeed between average and fast now comes down to the skill and experience of the sail trimmers and ability of the helmsman. Most sailors know the basic rules of setting up the headsail so that the windward tell-tales all lift together and keeping the mainsail top batten parallel to the end of the boom, but it is the next skill level up that separates the winners from the mid fleet pack.

The best way to trim a genoa is to have a picture in your mind's eye of how the sail should look in a particular wind strength, and then decide which of the four primary headsail shaping controls (sheet tension, car position, halyard tension, runner/backstay tension) needs to be adjusted to reach the target shape. The other vital point is that sail trim is a dynamic affair, and that the supposed state of 'perfect trim' changes continually with every pulse in wind speed and variation in wave size. This means that you can never sit back and say, 'This sail looks great,' because even if it does for that moment, the conditions will soon change slightly, requiring a matching alteration of trim. Knowing exactly when and by how much to change gear is the crucial factor, so let's start by looking at how to achieve the correct trim for medium air conditions for both sails, and then look at the changes necessary for light and heavy airs.

Trimming the genoa for medium airs

The trimmers should get to know the initial or mid-range lead position for each headsail on the boat and mark it on the track. This is so that when the sail goes up in the middle of a race the car position will not be far wrong and the sail can be set immediately. For the same reason, mark the lufftape of each sail with a strike mark which matches up with a reference point on the plastic headfoil that corresponds to a fast mid-range halyard setting. This can be vital when rounding the bottom mark in close company, when maximum speed is required to break free on the beat. If the genoa is hoisted with no guide as to how tight the luff is compared with the last upwind leg, it is too late to discover the fact when sheeted in and on the wind. Having to stop and luff the boat in order to tension the halyard at this stage could mean losing an overlap that you have just spent the last reaching leg trying to establish.

51

The degree of change in shape of the genoa entry as a result of tensioning the halyard will be determined by the fabric in the front end of the sail. Dacron genoas require around 150 mm of halyard tension before the entry will be noticeably affected, whereas a new Mylar sail will need only 30 mm and a Kevlar sail even less. Laminated sails are thus more responsive to small alterations in halyard, although their range of adjustment is limited. Beware of over-tensioning laminate sails, as permanent distortion can result. The latest developments in moulded sails are even more stable and fixed in their shape. Sails built to Sobstad Sailmakers' 'Genesis' and North Sails' '3 DL' patented construction systems have the draft rigidly fixed in the designed position, and halyard tension is necessary only to remove the wrinkles in the luff in medium winds and above. Tensioning the luff of a moulded sail further may serve to round up the entry slightly, but will have almost no effect on the draft position. They are more of a single shape sail, their benefits in performance stemming from their reduced weight and the reduction in distortion of the leech.

If racing a one-design class where the number of headsails is limited and genoas are therefore carried over a wide wind range, fit a simple genoa cunningham tackle which can be operated easily by the bowman from the rail, as is popular in J-24 class. This avoids the bother of trying to adjust the halyard from the middle of the boat and saves considerable wear on the halyard and sheave. However, it is not so suitable for boats which carry several headsails, as it means removing and re-attaching the cunningham every time there is a sail change.

Use the time before the race to sail upwind and fine tune the lead position and halyard tension for the actual wind and sea conditions. Start off by getting the helmsman to luff the boat gently and see how the weather tell-tales lift. If the upper tell-tale lifts first, it is an indication that there is too much twist in the top of the sail and that the leech needs to be sheeted harder, so move the car forward slightly and try the test again. You may find the tell-tales will never lift exactly together due to other factors, such as uneven positioning of the woolies, an un-fair luff curve on the headsail, or an uneven entry due to too much forestay sag.

The next step is to ask the helmsman if he or she is happy with the set up. He may feel he needs more power to get through the waves, so try tensioning the halyard some more, thus pulling the draft forward to create a more powerful shape. If the genoa has been cut on the flat side it may be necessary to power it up even more by letting the car forward and easing the sheet to maintain the same degree of twist. If the boat is struggling on pointing the helmsman may call for more leech tension or to tighten the runner. Use the upper spreader and the chainplates as a guide for setting up the leech. When the genoa is trimmed in all the way it should just touch these two points at the same time; if it doesn't, move the lead.

In light to medium conditions the leech should be fairly closed for maximum pointing ability. Once boatspeed is good, notice how far off the top spreader the genoa leech rests, so that the setting can be repeated each time you tack.

Having set up the lead position correctly and applied just enough halyard tension to remove the wrinkles from the luff, and trimmed the sheet in so that the leech is 60 mm off the spreader, the boat should be getting up to speed. Fine tuning from this initial set-up is now a matter of detective work. In order to go faster you need to find clues as to what it is that is making the sail slow. The first step is to identify the symptoms, such as a comparative low heading. It is important to pick up on these signs early, before you lose valuable distance to leeward.

Have one of the crew on the rail constantly monitor boatspeed and height against the boats around you. If he calls down that the speed is good but the pointing low, the helmsman will know he is probably sailing too low, or 'fat' as the latest jargon has it, and should trade some speed for height. The helm then needs to communicate to the trimmers what he is doing so they can trim for height accordingly.

If pointing is still below that of the rest of the fleet, it is time to try more runner tension (or backstay tension in the case of a masthead rig) to reduce the amount of forestay sag and fine up the genoa entry. Remember that the runner also tensions the genoa luff, so be ready to ease off the halyard tension slightly if a lot of runner is put on, otherwise the draft will be too far forward and will not help pointing ability.

Changes for light airs

When the windspeed drops a few knots the first and most important gear change to make is to ease the runner or backstay. If the wind drops from 14 to 10 knots on a fractional 40 footer, the reading on the load cell would typically want to go down from 5500 kgs to around 3000–2500 kgs. Reducing the tension in the forestay in this way is the quickest way to power the boat up, as it has four major effects on the rig at once:

1 The forestay falls away to leeward and astern, so adding depth to the genoa and creating a more powerful entry.
2 As a result of the above, the helmsman has a wider 'groove' to sail in, which will help to pick up speed. (A wide groove is provided by a rounded entry to the headsail and means that the helmsman can steer through a wider angle without stalling the sail. A narrow groove sail is one with a fine entry, and although it produces high pointing, it is akin to sailing on a knife edge.)
3 Genoa twist is reduced as a result of the aft rotation of the sail as the forestay sags off. This adds both feel on the helm and improves heading.
4 It adds depth to the middle of the mainsail as the mast straightens up.

The end result is that the helmsman should regain some feel on the helm and the trimmer will be able to generate more power from the genoa.

When the wind speed is less than 6 knots true, there is likely to be more friction at the water/air interface as a result of the laminar nature of airflow at this velocity (Fig 4.1) This means there can be considerable windshear within this boundary layer of a few metres above the surface. Hence the genoa needs extra twist in these conditions to match the change in apparent wind angle with height. So if boatspeed is still poor after easing the runner and deepening the sail, try twisting the top of the genoa some more by easing the sheet and/or moving the car aft. The top tell-tales should give you a clue as to the right setting. Above 6 knots, the theorists say laminar flow breaks up into turbulent airflow which creates more even vertical mixing and hence less windshear within the boundary layer; so reduce the twist and sheet the genoa in for pointing.

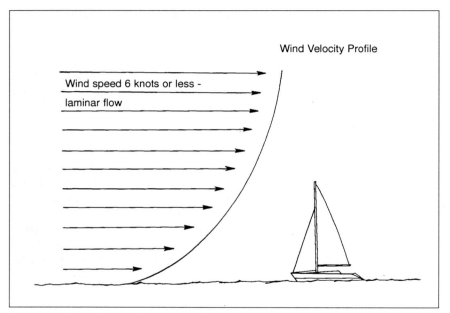

Fig 4.1 *When the wind speed is below 6 knots there is likely to be considerable friction between the air and water, due to the laminar nature of the air flow at this low velocity. This leads to noticeable wind shear within the boundary layer of a few metres above the surface.*

The worst speed sapping scenario is light airs and a choppy left over sea. Here you need a deep powerful headsail, with the backstay or runner well eased to power up the front of the genoa. On masthead boats check that there is enough slack in the backstay to really sag off the forestay. If the last race you did was in heavy air, the chances are that you will need to let off the bottlescrew above the hydraulic tensioner to slacken the forestay sufficiently. The helmsman may need to make relatively large alterations in course to steer around and over the waves, as in such little wind there will be no power to go through them – and once stopped by one it will take ages to build speed again. The genoa trimmer, likely to be sitting to leeward next to the winch, needs to follow the helmsman's course up and down on the wind. In light airs it is much quicker for the trimmer to react to each lift or header than it is to wait for the helmsman to slowly come up or bear down to meet them, and saves using excessive rudder. The helmsman may on occasion miss the odd lift, but the trimmer, concentrating hard on the front of the genoa, is the backup and should alert the driver by calling out 'I am trimming in to the lift', or just tell the helm to take the lift. Similarly with a heading shift; in very light winds the trimmer should ease the sheet to the header and communicate the fact to the helmsman so that he can slowly bear off to the new breeze without having to use a large amount of drag inducing tiller movement. The idea is to maintain the sails at the optimum angle to the wind the whole time in the shifting breeze, irrespective of the yacht's heading.

Keep a slight 10° heel to leeward to help fill the sails and to create more helm. This is perhaps the major factor to good light airs speed, as without good feel on the helm the boat will wander upwind, missing vital shifts and end up sailing a longer route to the mark.

Heavy airs headsail trim

As the wind builds towards the maximum windspeed for the heavy No 1 genoa the trimmers need to discuss when to change down to a smaller sail. The best indication of when to reduce sail comes from the speedo. The trimmers should know from past experience with the headsail what is the target speed for the current windspeed, or if new to the boat, should use a polar diagram to predict the target speed. (See Fig 5A, page 80). Thus, if you were achieving 7.1–7.3 knots with the heavy No 1 in 17 knots true, but only 6.8 knots in 22 knots of wind, then it is time to change to the next sail down.

A more obvious indication of the need to change headsail is the wholesale lifting of the front half of the main, due to the build up of pressure on the leeward side. The mainsheet trimmer will be having problems trying to de-power the sail, as he will not be able to drop the traveller far enough without the sail inverting. A small amount of backwind or 'bubble' near the luff is fine, but if half the main is lifting it is a sign that the airflow through the slot is too slow, so the pressure on the leeward side of the main builds up, causing the sail to invert. To cure the problem the genoa needs to exhaust more quickly: ie the air needs to pass through the slot faster, so move the car aft to flatten the middle of the genoa and twist the leech open. If this is not enough and the speed is still below target, it is time to change headsail.

At the bottom end of the wind range of a 100 per cent No 3 jib the sail is relatively under-powered and needs to be set deep with the leech firmly sheeted. The sail is then progressively flattened as the wind speed increases. A technique to try in 30 knots plus and big seas is to sheet the No 3 further outboard in order to sail fast and low. It is impossible to point high in such conditions so a better VMG can be obtained by sailing the boat flatter, faster and lower with the No 3 set wide and open in the top. In a Sigma 38 cruiser racer we used to sheet the 100 per cent jib in between the shrouds on to the very front of the 135 per cent genoa track, but reverted to the proper No 3 track in smoother water.

Trimming the mainsail

The two key elements to fast mainsail trim are:

- Having the mast set up correctly (which we have just discussed in Chapter 3).
- Taking on board the fact that the whole purpose of mainsail trim is to balance the helm and help steer the boat, rather than being

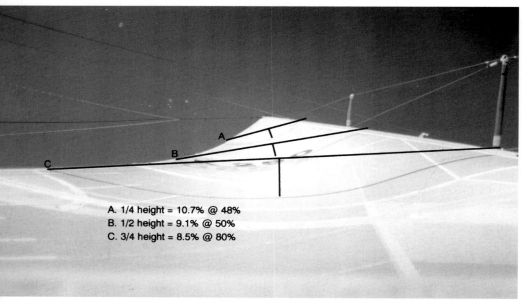

A. 1/4 height = 10.7% @ 48%
B. 1/2 height = 9.1% @ 50%
C. 3/4 height = 8.5% @ 80%

To check both the set-up and overall condition of your mainsail, take a photo like this with a wide angle lens, taking care to get both ends of the trim stripe in. Draw the chord lines on and then measure off the depth and draft (see text). Thus for this Mylar mainsail on a half tonner sailing at 12 knots the shape is described as: 10.7% depth at 48% aft of the luff (draft position) for the top 1/4 height; 9.1% at 50% 1/2 height; and 8.5% at 50% at the bottom stripe. The genoa can be measured in exactly the same way.

purely a matter of harnessing as much sailpower as possible. What this means is that the mainsail trimmer has to learn not to be too greedy, and that as the wind strength gets up, the boat becomes faster with a flatter, more twisted and less powerful main which creates less drag.

Setting the mainsail for medium air

Sailing in a wind band of between 8–16 knots true, the boat should be fully powered up with the draft position at 50 per cent aft and the depth set fairly deep at the bottom of the wind band, flattening off a little over 12 knots. These depth and draft percentages will obviously very from sail to sail, depending on what shape your sail was designed to be originally, but they serve as a guideline. The depth percentages show how a sail should always be some 2–3 per cent flatter in the bottom third and slightly fuller in the top. The draft position of 50 per cent back from the luff is the optimal position for pointing ability, but in a short chop it may pay to drag the draft forward to around 48 per cent for more speed and less height.

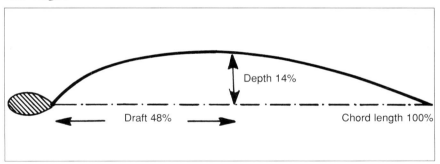

Fig 4.2 *Depth and draft.*

Just like learning to sight the rig, reading the mainsail's depth and draft is a matter of training your eye. Look up the sail from under the middle of the boom and, eyeing the trim stripes, try to decide where along the stripe the greatest depth lies; this is the draft position (See Fig 4.2). The easiest way to judge the position is to divide the trim stripe into two, and then decide if the draft lies in front or aft of this point: ie more or less than 50 per cent. The only way to gain a more accurate measure of the depth and draft is to photograph the sail, tilting the camera to get both ends of the lower trim stripe in the shot. Draw the chord line in from where the trim stripe intersects the luff and leech. Then with one edge of a set square on the chord line, and a ruler resting against another, carefully slide the set square along the ruler until the set square is resting on the last (and there-fore deepest) part of the curve. Mark this point and then construct a perpendicular from there up to the chord line. The length of this line that you have just drawn represents the maximum depth of the sail at that section, and the point at which it cuts the chord line is the draft position. The only way to measure the depth is in percentage terms, as it is impossible to measure absolute values from photographs. Measure the depth line and express it as a percentage of the total chord length. The draft position is recorded in a similar fashion: just measure back from the luff to the maximum depth line and convert the number into a percentage of the total chord length from luff to leech. Thus in Fig 4.2 the depth is described as 14 per cent at 48 per cent aft.

In order to get the boat pointing high in medium airs, the boom should be sheeted as close to the centreline as possible. Most sail trim books tell you to balance the helm with the traveller, which is quite correct but the trap some helmsmen fall into is in asking the mainsail trimmer to ease the car down the track whenever he is struggling for speed. This is often when the wind speed suddenly drops or the boat is slowed by waves. Easing the traveller only serves to ease pressure on the helm and reduce pointing ability, as it is the same as moving the genoa leads outboard. Dropping the traveller down in order to foot off and sail low is fine, but to do so whilst keeping the same heading is not so fast. Depending on how the mainsheet system is organised, easing the traveller without adjusting the mainsheet on many boats actually results in tightening the leech. So, at the very moment the helmsman requires more speed he is in fact giving away height, closing up the main, stalling it further, with little increase in boatspeed. Far better to leave the boom on the centreline and ease the main fine tune to twist open the top leech a little more to match the reduced wind speed. The rule is the same as for trimming the genoa when the wind is going down; twist the sail some more. As soon as the boat is up to speed squeeze the main in to regain height again and watch to see if the speed remains good.

It helps to hold the boom on the centreline in this way as long as possible, balancing the helm with the twist so that optimum height can be maintained, especially with a fractional rig. De-powering from the top of the sail first helps to reduce heeling forces and keeps the boat flat and fast. The twist will also reduce drag in the top of the sail.

As soon as there is enough breeze to hike the boat out the mainsail can be trimmed in for optimum VMG. The starting point for trimming the leech is to line up the outboard end of the top batten with the end of the boom, and use that as a relative comparison. A more open leech setting would see the end of the batten pointing to leeward of the boom and the most closed it should ever be is parallel to the boom or slightly angled to windward in flat water. Masthead rigs can be squeezed a little higher as the training effect of the headsail reaches all the way up the mainsail, whilst the fractional rig is faster with more twist due to the lack of genoa bending the flow around the back of the main above the hounds.

Strike marks stuck along the trim stripes make it easier to assess the draft positions.

The depth of the mainsail is controlled in the top two thirds by mast bend (ie runner and checkstay tension) and in the base by the outhaul. The sail should be set at its maximum designed depth when the boat is under-powered and then progressively flattened once the boat becomes over-pressed. The outhaul should be pulled on all the way to the black band as soon as there is 8–10 knots of breeze and only eased when lacking power in light and lumpy conditions. Adjusting the outhaul can also be a way of reducing or creating helm as required. Tensioning the foot of the sail opens up the lower leech, forcing the lower batten open. A closed lower leech will noticeably add helm to the boat.

On a fractional boat, runner tension is used primarily to shape the genoa and to effect pointing, and has a secondary effect upon mainsail depth. This is the reason why it is vital the mast bend and luff curve match. As the breeze gets up keep a check on the draft position to ensure it does not move too far aft under load. Sight up from under the middle of the boom, as you would to take a photo, and estimate if the draft lies forward of the 50 per cent position. Some race boats have diamonds or strike marks stuck along the trim stripes to indicate the 50 per cent draft position, and even 25 per cent and 75 per cent positions to aid quick appraisal (see photo on page 59). The draft will slip aft more rapidly in an old, tired sail, so use the cunningham to pull the draft forward, back to where it should be, around 48–50 per cent.

It is impossible to recommend here how much checkstay should be used for a particular wind strength, as it depends on the depth of the main, the mainsail fabric, and the amount of mast bend. The checkstay is used to pull the middle of the mast straight in order to add depth to that section, and can help to keep a flexible spar in column, so maintaining rig tension. Dacron mainsails will obviously stretch deeper as the sail is loaded up, so the mainsail should be cut flatter than a laminate sail and the checkstays used earlier to power up the main in light airs. It can then be eased once the sail starts to stretch deeper, in turn removing the excess depth by mast bend. Try to learn at what wind speed the checkstay comes on and then off for your mainsail. Choppy wave conditions will demand more power and hence more checkstay tension.

Light airs mainsail trim

In very light conditions the key to good upwind speed is to keep the top of the mainsail working. We have already seen that below 6 knots there can be considerable windshear in the surface layers, so comparable twist will be required in the main.

Pull the traveller car as far as possible to windward and temporarily tie off any part of the mainsheet system which pulls vertically down to the centre of the boat, to prevent closing the leech. With the boom on the centreline and minimal downward tension on the mainsheet, the leech will be encouraged to twist open and the leech streamers to fly, indicating the leech is not stalled. At such low wind speeds the initial goal is to generate airflow across the sail and worry about height later. Keep twisting the sail until the upper leech streamer flies, and then gently trim on until it almost collapses. If the weight of the boom closes the leech and prevents flow, you need to find a way of lifting it up. The best solution is a solid strut kicker (or rigid vang) capable of upward pressure. The alternative is a spare halyard clipped on to the end of the boom. This option can be a problem when you come to tack as the halyard has to be removed and changed over before each tack. I have even won races with a broom propped up under the boom, as the difference between the leech working and not working is like night and day.

In light airs you need a relatively deep, draft forward shape in the sail with a straight, freely exhausting leech. Straighten the mast up to deepen the sail to around 15 per cent at 45 per cent, 16 per cent at 45 per cent and 18 per cent at 45 per cent at the 1/4, 1/2 and 3/4 heights respectively. Ease off the checkstay if the sail becomes too full in the luff and let the pre-bend remove the excess cloth.

The mainsheet trimmer needs to remember to change the top batten for a softer version if the forecast is light. With the proliferation of full-length top battens, too stiff a batten in light air can force too much depth into the head of the sail since there will be insufficient leech load to lever it open. The other problem with too stiff a batten can be that the induced tension can cause the top of the sail to catch on the backstay, requiring the leech to be jerked several times before the sail sets on the new tack.

Heavy air trim

As soon as the boat becomes over-powered and the amount of helm is more than 5°, it is time to redress the helm balance. As the breeze builds, the order of de-powering I tend to use goes something like this:

1 Pull the cunningham on hard. This pulls the draft back to around 50 per cent or further forward if more power is required. A secondary effect is to open the top leech, reducing helm, heeling forces and drag.
2 Tension the outhaul as hard as it will go, flattening the base and opening the lower leech to reduce helm.
3 Ease the traveller down the track to balance the helm. Rather than keep having to ask the helmsman how much helm he has or have him calling when to dump the traveller, just watch to see what angle the tiller is at. It is helpful to mark 5° angles on the deck directly below the tiller to indicate the optimum helm, or use coloured tape on the top of the wheel to show when 5° of rudder angle is reached.
4 Wind the runner on hard and ease the checkstay for maximum mast bend to flatten the sail and ease the leech.
5 Sheet the mainsail hard enough to 'blade out' the top and prevent the sail from inverting and the leech from flogging. This will be quite hard, especially if sailing with a Dacron sail, as there will be a lot of elastic stretch to take up. However, Mylar or Kevlar mains tend to set themselves, in that if the balance between traveller position and mainsheet tension is not right the sail will invert and not set at all. Just use enough mainsheet to keep the sail set and the leech contributing lift. Too much leech tension will only add drag, helm and heel.
6 On a fractional rig pull on the backstay enough to open the top leech and de-power further. Again, be careful not to use so much backstay that the last few inches of the leech flog. What we are trying to achieve in heavy air is a flat, 'bladed out' mainsail, with up to the front third lifting or inverting, but with the leech still driving and generating lift. If this vital aft section of the leech stops working and the sail inverts totally, all flow across the sail breaks down, lift is lost, the drag factor goes up and the yacht slides rapidly to leeward.
7 Once the traveller has been dumped all the way down the track and the boat is still on its ear the boom somehow has to be let out further but

without losing leech tension, which we have just seen is vital for maintaining lift off the sail. The answer, if your kicker is strong enough, is to 'vang sheet'. This technique was developed amongst the competitive one-design classes such as the J-24 and Sigma 38, which carry a full main high up the wind range but are blessed with only a short mainsail track. Vang sheeting involves taking up considerable tension on the kicker, such that when the mainsheet is eased the kicker takes over holding the leech loading and the mainsheet simply serves to control the angle of the boom. Vang sheeting is fast upwind as it considerably reduces the load on the mainsheet, enabling the trimmer to alternately trim and then ease the main rapidly in response to each gust, so keeping the boat on its feet and the keel working to create lift. However, make sure all the kicker fittings and the boom are strong enough to take the load; the boom may well require an internal sleeve at the vang take-off point. Beware also of compressing a rod kicker too much so that the sliding tube 'bottoms out', as it can bend a rigid vang. It is important to ensure someone is detailed to ease the kicker before bearing off at the windward mark, otherwise the boom thrust could easily break the mast at the gooseneck.

8 At some stage the mainsail will be faster with a reef taken in. The exact timing of the reef will depend on:

- the amount of heel and helm.
- the headsail options available. Would the boat be faster with the No 4 and full main or No 3 and a reef?
- wave conditions. You can hang on to a full mainsail longer in flat water.
- the competition nearby. With a close rival on your hip you may lose a vital overlap if you go for the reef.
- distance to go to the windward mark. Would you lose more than you would gain if thee is only a short way to go to the mark?

A rigid vang makes taking in a reef much easier and quicker, as the boom does not fall down and flog about dangerously. Another speed saving tip is to use two rope clutches in line on the main halyard. Ease the halyard through the aftermost clutch first to a pre-marked spot which coincides with the reefed halyard position and pull the slack out between the two clutches. When the crew is ready to take in a quick reef, the forward clutch is thrown off and the reef point can be smartly hooked on with no fear of too much halyard coming down and then having to be winched up again.

Go faster techniques

One method of going faster in light airs can be carried out on the dock. If the forecast is light winds and the race a short inshore job, go through the boat from stem to stern and remove all excess gear that will not be needed that day; such as the No 4 genoa, the 1.5 oz kite, all the crew's oilskin trousers, boots, lunch, spare sheets, etc. You will be surprised at the weight that can be left ashore and the amount of unnecessary gear that accumulates in a boat over the season. Be careful not to remove any safety equipment that is required by the sailing instructions for that regatta. If racing under a cruiser racer handicap rule (CHS, IMS or PHRF) the removal of some items of accommodation may invalidate the rating, such as bunk cushions and salon tables. If you are unsure of what can be legally removed the simple test is to see if the boat was originally weighed with the item in place. If so, then it has to stay aboard. If you see another boat removing gear which has to be carried, a quiet word with one of the crew is usually enough to send them scurrying back down below with the relevant piece of furniture.

A harder decision to make on the morning of a light air race is if any of the crew are to be left ashore. Carefully check the wording of the sailing instructions that crew numbers can be changed during the series. Under the Channel Handicap System, the race committee have the option to allow a variation in crew numbers from the number that competed in the opening race of +2 or −2 for a crew of 5–12, or −3 and +2 for a crew of 13–20. The IMS rule has a declared crew weight limit, but no minimum crew requirement. If there are a couple of 'B-max' crew that are just along for their weight, this should be made clear at the beginning of the regatta so that they do not expect to sail on the light days. I have sailed boats where keen young guys have been upset to be asked to get off the boat just as she slips out from the dock. You cannot expect them to be keen and enthusiastic for the rest of the week after being treated like that.

Whatever loose equipment does remain on the boat – spare sails, anchor, chain and warps – should be stacked in the middle of the boat near the keel. In light and lumpy conditions any crew not involved in trimming the sails should be asked to sit to leeward downstairs, level with the keel, in an effort to reduce pitching. The downside to the modern breed of highly stiff IMS designs is that in such light and lumpy conditions some boats can be left 'hobby horsing' up and down and it can take longer to accelerate out of a tack, due to so much of the ballast being in a deep, bulb keel. Again 'indoor sailing' is never very popular with those who have to sit below on long hot days, but they should realise it is an important job and the best contribution to boatspeed that they can make at that moment, given the conditions. I once raced an IMS 33 footer in an autumn series where the owner and his son flew in from Germany for each race. One Sunday they spent the entire race below decks, saw nothing of the action, but were delighted when their new boat scored a first place. We have all had to serve our time below!

In light winds rig tension can be eased slightly on yachts where this can be easily achieved to relieve compression. In the case of a cruiser racer rig with swept back spreaders, easing the lowers a couple of turns will let more pre-bend into the mast and so reduce the depth of the main. Consider adding some extra rake by adding a 60 mm toggle to the forestay if there has been a previous problem of lack of helm in these conditions.

Speeding up the tacks

To speed up the boat through the tack in light airs sheet the main in rapidly as the helm goes over, to help kick the transom round to leeward. The temporary 'extra' helm aids the helmsman to get back on to the wind, but as soon as the boat is back on track ease the traveller and fine tune to build speed again. When tacking in medium and heavy airs, leave the traveller part way to leeward until the trimmer has settled the genoa, everyone is up on the rail, and the boat is back up to speed before trimming in the leech. Have a spare crew member in the middle of the boat to call the speed through the tack to save the trimmers having to look at the knotmeter when they need to be looking up at and trimming their respective sails.

5. Going Faster Downwind

The downwind legs are the real fun part of yacht racing. They bring a release from the strain and tension of hiking out upwind, and in a decent breeze the opportunity for exciting, high speed sailing. There is a greater potential for place changes downwind, especially on the run, where reading the shifts correctly, choosing the right side of the course, and a few well timed gybes can bring a recovery that even Lazarus would be proud of.

But why does downwind sail trim often appear to be such a mysterious art? Why do boats occasionally fly straight past for no apparent reason, and why do you sometimes find conflicting opinions amongst a crew as to how the spinnaker should be trimmed?

One answer is because few sailors or even the experts understand completely how flow around a spinnaker behaves and therefore find it hard to picture exactly what shape they are trying to achieve when setting the sail to best advantage in each condition. Some of the top race boat trimmers seem to have an intuitive feel for getting the best out of the chute, but I believe you can develop your feel for kite trimming by studying the subject, learning a few main principles and then gaining as much experience as you can in a wide variety of wind conditions.

Another reason for this air of mystery is that it is not always obvious when the trim is wrong offwind. Upwind, if the mainsail is not set up right it can be all too evident, with big creases running across the sail. Downwind there are infinitely more possible combinations than on the beat. In other words, there are many more opportunities to get it wrong downwind, due mainly to the free flying and hence less controllable nature of a spinnaker.

It is well worth looking at how the air flow around a spinnaker behaves in order to appreciate how the sail controls work to affect and change the shape (see Fig 5.1).

Unlike a mainsail or headsail, where the object is to keep flow attached over the majority of the sail, a spinnaker has flow attached over only 50 per cent of its area on a beam reach. Dead running, the sail is stalled completely, which is why running is the slowest point of sail. The trimmer's aim is to get some flow established and try to maintain it. Fig 5.2 shows why over trimming the kite is disastrous, as any attached flow will be stalled immediately. The rule is always: if in doubt let it out.

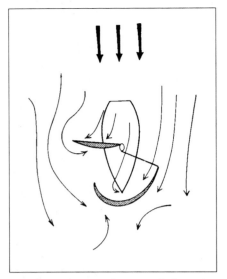

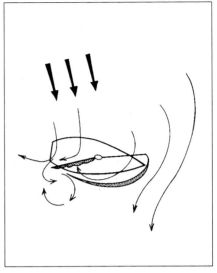

Fig 5.1 *Running downwind the spinnaker is almost completely stalled. Fly the sail as far away from the rig as possible to allow the sail to exhaust freely and minimise disturbance to the mainsail.*

Fig 5.2 *Overtrimming the spinnaker stalls out any attached flow over both the spinnaker and mainsail.*

Perfecting the bear-away spinnaker set

The very first opportunity to gain ground downwind is during the spinnaker hoist. It is amazing how much shouting goes on aboard some boats, as all the pent-up emotion and often frustration from the upwind leg is vented on the poor souls hoisting the kite. What is required is a close, controlled rounding of the mark with the spinnaker popping open as soon as the bow turns away from the wind. Hoisting and gybing the spinnaker are the two most labour intensive manoeuvres in yacht racing, and demand the closely co-ordinated efforts of every single member of the team.

Approaching the windward mark, either the navigator/tactician or the genoa trimmer should move to leeward to call the distance into the mark, just like calling the count down to the start. This allows each of the crew to concentrate on the timing of their own job without having to look for the mark, thus avoiding a mad rush to ease sheets, load the winch with the kite sheets etc. Whoever is sitting to leeward also needs to advise the unsighted helmsman if he is laying the mark and when to begin bearing off. The mainsheet trimmer needs this information too, so that he can ease the traveller down the track to allow the helmsman to bear off. He also needs advance warning to enable him to get the course mainsheet control

The spinnaker guy can be sneaked back behind the genoa, timed so that the tack of the spinnaker is at the pole end just as the hoist is called.

out of the jammer in anticipation of letting out the main.

Once the tactician is confident the mark can be laid without any further tacks, he calls for the pole to be raised. This is carried out either by the bowman or the mastman raising the pole up the mast to a preset mark; the bowman then lifts up the outboard end to horizontal. The pitman tails the pole uphaul (or topping lift), ideally by leaning in from his hiking position on the rail. A few lengths from the mark the cockpit crew prepares the sheet and guys, by pulling through the slack and loading the winches. For a close beam reach in a breeze, lead the sheet to the windward cabin top winch in order to keep the weight of the trimmer and grinder on the high side.

A length from the mark the pole should be set at the expected angle for the reach and the correct height for the wind strength and fixed solid in place by tensioning the up and downhauls. The spinnaker guy can then be sneaked back, behind the genoa, timed so that the tack of the kite is at the pole end the second the hoist is called. As the foot of the sail is being stretched out in the lee of the headsail, it should not fill until the genoa is cast off. In breezy conditions the bowman should stay to leeward with his hand on the spinnaker bag in case the kite decides to blow away early and wrap itself around the mark. If any part of the spinnaker does brush the mark as the boat goes round it is classed as part of the boat and requires a 360° turn in exoneration. If heavy vang tension has been used on the beat, remember to let half of it off before easing sheets to aid bearing off (and avoid breaking the mast!)

One trick to speed up the bear away is to hold the genoa sheet in as the main is eased, so that the bow is blown round to leeward. This technique allows less rudder to be used and so should speed up your exit from the mark. As soon as it is safe to bear off, taking into account the tidal flow, the tactician should give clearly the word for the hoist. The mastman quickly hoists the halyard, hand over hand at the mast, and on large masthead rigs may need a hand from the bowman to get the last few metres up. If he shouts out when the sail is two metres from the top, the trimmers will know when to start taking in the sheet; but not before hand, as it will load up the sail and prevent it from going up. The guy, however, should be hauled back as soon as the hoist is called, as it does not act to fill the sail on its own and helps to avoid wraps. If the timing is right, the head of the spinnaker should reach the mast just as the pole is squared back and the sheet comes in to fill the sail. The genoa should come down immediately and ideally be bagged or secured with a sail tie and unclipped from the forestay, then brought back to the mast so that the weight of the wet sail is not left on the fore deck. As soon as the wind angle is aft of around 110°, the rig should automatically be pulled forward by hooking up the genoa halyard to the tack fitting and winding the halyard up tight, just so that the mast does not quite invert. Moving the rig forward in this way raises the height of the sail plan and in doing so removes the effects of mast rake which are not so beneficial downwind.

The gybe set

The main point for crews to remember when attempting a gybe hoist is that nothing can be hoisted until the boat has gybed and is back on its feet. This means that before the pole can be fully raised (the mast end can of course be raised into position on the mast and the outboard end left resting on the deck) the headsail has to be gybed over and sheeted on the new side. The mastman should begin the hoist as soon as the main is gybed. If the genoa is left billowing out on the new gybe, the kite will go straight up into it and will be prevented from filling quickly. Do not forget either in the excitement of the mark rounding to put some tension on the new runner, because if the spinnaker fills with a bang in a stiff breeze, it may just snap a lightweight racing mast at the hounds if there is nothing to pull against the halyard load.

If you use rubber bands or wool 'stops' on the chute, then it can be hoisted on the windward side before the gybe, which obviously speeds things up, and can be a good idea on big masthead rigs where there is more sail to hoist and hence a greater chance of a wrap. As soon as the yacht has gybed, the pole is raised and the guy clipped in. Because there

The genoa should come down and be removed from the fore deck as soon as the spinnaker is hoisted, so that the weight of the sail is not left on the fore deck, where it can catch and hold water.

is no time to preset the pole, the guy needs to come back as soon as the hoist is called, breaking open the stops to avoid any twists or wraps.

Well before the windward mark the navigator needs to advise the helmsman of the bearing to steer on the reach and how broad or shy the angle will be. The crew boss then passes the information forward to the front of the boat, so the crew knows the correct height and approximate angle to position the pole, and in conjunction with an appraisal of wind speed will also know the sort of rig loads to expect. If the whole crew can thus anticipate how close the reach will be the boat can be set up accordingly. In very light air with a 120° wind angle this may mean hoisting the sail with a lightweight sheet attached and setting the spinnaker pole low. Conversely, before a 95° reach in 24 knots the crew will ensure the tweaker line is completely let off, the mastman is ready with the vang in his hand and the weight is up on the rail straight after the hoist in order to keep the boat flat.

Going fast on the reach

If the next leg is a windy reach, the crew's weight should immediately hit the rail with their legs out and bodies well aft. The pitman needs to twist inboard to keep his eye on the main, his ear tuned to the main trimmer

On a close reach, when a gust hits, concentrate on hiking the boat flat and if the boat remains level it will accelerate rather than heel to leeward and stall.

and his hand on the kicker line, ready to throw it off if a broach threatens.

Close reaching with the apparent wind around 90°, the kite is best over squared slightly to flatten off the sail and the pole kept low in order to tension the luff and so induce the leech to twist off. This allows the sail to exhaust more freely which results in more attached flow across the sail, less drag, less heeling forces and hence more speed; just like twisting open the genoa. As a gust strikes it is important to ease as much spinnaker sheet as possible without the sail collapsing, so as to keep the boat on the level and travelling fast.

At the same time the mainsail trimmer needs to ease a lot of sheet in a hurry. Because of the number of purchases involved in a block and tackle mainsheet system it is often impossible to do so fast enough, so the main trimmer needs to take the mainsheet in his hand straight from the last block on the boom with plenty of slack mainsheet pulled through ready to be dumped in an instant. If the boat has a long mainsheet track which runs easily, this can be used instead in medium air; but in gusty conditions you need to make sure the mainsail can be immediately let right out to the shrouds to save the boat from broaching.

When a gust is of sufficient force that the helmsman cannot hold the boat on track, all the power needs to be dumped from the main rather than just easing it, by letting go the kicker. It is vital that the crew operate these controls whilst still keeping their weight outboard or they will only compound the problem. One of the crew on the rail should be concentrating on calling the gusts, so the helmsman has warning to bear off and the kite trimmer has notice to ease the sheet in time, before becoming overpowered.

Once you have experienced a really windy reach in complete control; where the main is flogged and the kite eased right out but not collapsed, when the crew lean out rather than in to release control lines, then you will feel a lot more confident. The difference between a yacht which is knocked flat and stalls and one that stays flat and gets up and planes is incredible. Boatlengths can be gained in seconds. On a heavy airs reach, confidence and slick crew work is the key to success.

A few other performance enhancing techniques to try for close reaching include:

- Ease the spinnaker halyard out 30 cm so that the kite flies further away from the rig.
- Keep the mainsail flattened off the same as for upwind.
- Have all the crew move aft and hike out hard.
- Keep the pole low.
- Let the spinnaker tweaker line right off so that the main boom becomes the only limiting factor on spinnaker clew height. Some keelboats, such as the Soling, allow the spinnaker sheet to ride up over the end of the boom, to encourage the spinnaker leech to twist off. Getting hold of the sheet for the take down can be a bit of a problem though.

White sail reaching

If the breeze heads there will soon come a point where the boat will be faster and higher with a genoa flying, rather than a strapped spinnaker. In anticipation of this, the thinking crew will already have attached the snatch block to the toe rail or pad eye, a little way forward of the upwind car position and as far outboard as possible. A reaching sheet with a snap shackle on the end is clipped on to the sail and can be led straight to a cabin top winch, pulling the sail outboard and forward. Such arrangements are always a compromise, as the correct sheeting position for this wind angle is about one metre outboard of the boat. However, through a combination of outboard lead and genoa sheet the sail can be trimmed fairly well on the tell-tales. The upper leech will always appear too open, so expect the top tell-tale to lift before the rest. In strong winds the trimmer will need to sit to windward and forward enough to see the front of the headsail, so leave a single turn around the primary winch and take the tail up to the windward halyard winch and trim from the high side.

The gybe

The gybe is undoubtedly the hardest manoeuvre to do well on the race course. The reason is simply because it relies upon the closely co-ordinated efforts of almost the entire crew, and if one member manages to get it not quite right, then the efforts of the rest of the crew are wasted.

Gybing on the run

The easiest gybe to effect is dead downwind in light to medium airs. Here the most important priority is to keep the spinnaker flying throughout the gybe. If the loads are light enough one trimmer standing in the middle of the cockpit should take both sheet and guy in his hands and gently float the kite around the fore stay in time with the bowman. One person will always co-ordinate the sheet and guy better than two. In light airs the mainsheet trimmer can help by holding the mainsail on the centreline for a few seconds as the boom goes over in order to reduce the chances of the spinnaker collapsing from being in the lee of the main.

On smaller yachts that use the end-for-end gybing technique it is important that the fore deck crew unclips the pole from the mast first, then from off the guy, before attaching the pole to the new guy. If not, there is a point at which the spinnaker pole is connected to both sheet and guy and the two clews of the sail are pulled in together which at best is slow and hard work for the bowman; and at worst will collapse the kite and in heavy air can cause the boat to roll dramatically.

On fractionally rigged boats there is often the added complication of taking up and letting off the runners. The runner operators need to be pretty sharp in a breeze, as if the mainsail is pinned in by the old runner the boat can be knocked flat. If too quick in letting it off, you could be waving goodbye to the mast over the front of the boat. In light airs it is not so important; anyone spare can throw off the old runner tail, but in a good breeze it is vital to have two people on the job. One should take up the tension on the new runner as the old one is cast off. Keep a little tension on the permanent backstay as a safety measure. Again, if the mainsheet trimmer can hold the mainsheet amidships for a second it will ease the operation. He will not be able to hold the mainsheet by hand, so with the traveller cleated in the middle, sheet the main all the way in as the boom comes over, hold it there until the leeward runner starts to come off before then letting it all run out. In medium airs I tend to centre the traveller before the gybe and then just grab the mainsheet and throw it across the boat. This makes for a quick gybe and avoids being caught by a gust with the main pinned in, but take great care that no arms, legs or heads are in the path of the sheet or boom. A shout of, 'Heads', just before the boom crashes over serves as a useful reminder.

Reach to reach gybing

Probably the toughest type of gybe to carry out is from a reach to reach using the end-for-end technique with single sheet and guy. Here the team-work is crucial for a slick gybe and goes something like this:

Helmsman: Approaches the mark slightly high, so as to make room in which to bear off to make the gybe easier.

Cockpit: Pulls down windward tweaker (twinning line) to bring the sheet closer to the bowman's reach. Eases the guy forward to a preset mark which represents a pole position just off the fore stay. Lets off just enough downhaul (fore guy) so that the bowman does not have a struggle to get the pole back on to the mast.

Bowman: Braces himself strongly by facing forward with his shoulder lean-ing hard against the mast and feet locked solid. As the boat bears off into the gybe, the compression on the spinnaker pole is reduced, making it

When gybing on the run the most important pri-ority is to keep the spin-naker flying throughout the gybe. Photo: *Christel Clear*

easier to unclip the pole from the mast. He then fires the outboard end free, swings the pole across the boat, leans across and forces the new guy into the pole end, pushes the pole out and leans back against the mast to help gain the last push to get the pole back on to the mast.

Cockpit: Releases the leeward tweaker as soon as the old guy is unclipped from the pole. Tensions the fore guy the second the pole is back on the mast which helps pull the pole forward and up to the clew of the sail.

Trimmer: Takes the new sheet up to windward and sheets in as the boat comes up on to the second reaching leg. The problems occur when the helmsman turns the boat too fast and the bowman is unable to get the pole up on to the mast before the sail loads up on the new gybe. The cockpit crew should be watching like a hawk throughout the manoeuvre, to ensure he has enough slack at the right time and that his timing coincides with the action on the fore deck.

Dip-pole gybing

The dip-pole gybe with twin sheets and guys is used on larger yachts from about 30 foot upwards By its nature it involves higher loads and hence more crew, so increasing the possibilities for errors.

Many crews, in apprehension of the gybe, forget to square the pole sufficiently, which means that as the boat bears off and the apparent wind swings aft the spinnaker becomes hidden behind the main and collapses. The pole needs to be squared back in sympathy with the helmsman steering into the gybe. Novice helmsmen tend to steer a little too slowly into the gybe and are sometimes scared to point the boat dead downwind. As a result the mainsail remains loaded up and is hard to pull across, so delaying the gybe. The secret is to steer relatively quickly but smoothly on to a dead run, hold the boat there as the boom comes over and then head up to help the kite to fly as the pole is set on the windward side. As the fore deck work improves the helmsman should steer straight through the gybe without pausing, irrespective of what is happening to the fore deck. Again, it is vital that the two kite trimmers watch the progress on the fore deck to aid, rather than fight the actions of the bowman.

The simple answer to improving gybing is to practise again and again. Begin with nice slow gybes on the run, to sort out technique and co-ordination and then speed it up to try to heat up the angles. With each person concentrating on his own job it can be hard to see exactly where a gybe is going wrong, so ask the tactician to stand at the back of the boat and observe the whole operation to see where any problems may lie.

There is no feeling on earth like a perfectly executed gybe when surfing on the top of a wave in 25 knots, while all the boats around you crash and burn. With good technique, a bit of practice, and steady nerves that could be you!

Running faster

As the kite goes up and the crew settles down on the run, the tendency is for everyone to relax and unwind from the upwind leg. But the run should be viewed as an attacking leg, an ideal opportunity to get back from an indifferent beat. The correct set up for the boat is in many cases diametrically opposite to that required for windward work, so the crew need to immediately begin resetting the controls.

The rig needs to be pulled forward by clipping the genoa halyard on to the tack fitting as soon as the sail hits the deck and should be done as a matter of course on the run. The pitman carefully winds it back to either a pre-marked position on the halyard or to the call of the mastman who looks up the rig to check that the mast is not wound forward so much that it inverts. Obviously this trick is of greatest benefit on a heavily raked fractional rig where the top of the mast may move forward up to 1.5 metres. This removes the negative effects of the aft rake which improves feel upwind but does nothing for boatspeed downwind. Instead, raking the mast forward on the run lifts the whole sail plan vertically, away from the layers of surface friction and into faster air flow and also helps create a greater projected area. It is also worth trying on a masthead rigged boat but the benefits will not be so great as the movement of the mast will be limited by the amount of adjustment in the backstay. One of the 'afterguard' should have the job of checking that the backstay and runners are let off as the rig is taken forward. On an in-line fractional rig take a couple of turns on the runner winch just to give the mast some support and stop it from shaking around in the waves.

In light airs downwind, the objective is to sail a course that gives you the optimum VMG (velocity made good) to the mark. The kite trimmer is in the best position to feel when there is good pressure in the sail, enabling the helmsman to sail the boat a little lower and straighter to the mark. Conversely, when the trimmer feels the sheet go light he should call to the helm to come up a little to bring the apparent wind forward and increase the pressure on the spinnaker.

As there is seemingly such a 'wide groove' to sail in offwind, the choice of which is the fastest angle to sail can be a difficult one, especially in an offshore race where the wind is likely to change during the leg or in a mixed fleet where boats will be sailing at different VMGs. A set of polar numbers or a polar diagram specifically generated for your yacht can be useful here to suggest what angle to sail and the target speed for every wind strength. (See page 82). Alternatively, an instrument that gives a read-out of VMG can be used to find the angle that gives the highest value of VMG before it begins to decrease.

Downwind mainsail trim

Some mainsail trimmers simply let the sail out, knock off the cunningham, ease the outhaul and just leave the sail to rest against the spreaders, thinking there is little else to do. In fact trimming the main effectively downwind can bring just as great a reward in improved boatspeed as upwind.

Stiff laminate mainsails are a lot harder to read downwind than Dacron sails, and the old maxim of 'Let it out until the front flaps', is now a little out of date. I like to fit a couple of tell-tales on the sail around the two-thirds height and about 30 per cent aft of the luff and use them to find the best position for the main. I also find a row of three tell-tales just above the top batten is useful on the reach to indicate if the flow off the back of the mainsail is stalled at all. If the leeward ones start lifting or if the leech streamer is bent round to windward, it is a desperate cry for the top leech to be loosened off. The trimmer should keep the mainsheet in his hand and play it in response to each pulse in wind speed, each change in apparent wind angle and to every alteration in course.

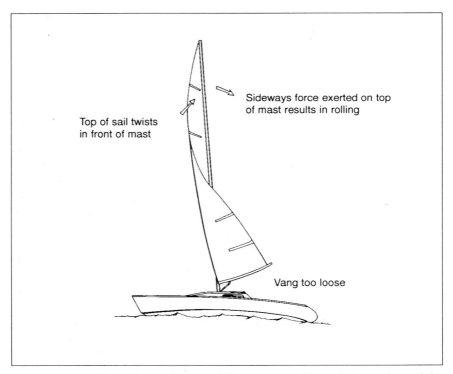

Top of sail twists in front of mast

Sideways force exerted on top of mast results in rolling

Vang too loose

Fig 5.3 *Aim to keep the top batten of the main at 90° to the centreline of the boat, otherwise it will twist in front of the mast and sideways forces can result, causing the boat to roll violently from side to side.*

Many boats release the outhaul too far in medium to heavy air, maybe 250 mm, which only serves to reduce the sail's projected area. In strong winds I would leave it out at the black band.

When there is enough breeze to run low the mainsail should be let right out to the shrouds and the vang constantly adjusted to match the fluctuations in wind speed. The aim is to keep the top batten parallel to the end of the boom which should ideally be at 90° to the centreline. Trying to set the correct twist more through mainsheet tension means that the lower third of the main will be too far in and reducing the sail effective area. If the vang is strapped down too tight the top batten will be hooked up to windward, stalling any flow off the top of the sail. Take a look back at Fig 5.1 which shows the majority of the sail plan is stalled dead downwind anyway and so it is important for boatspeed to nurture any flow across the sail. Conversely, if the vang is too slack and the leech allowed to twist round in front of the mast, not only is the projected area lost, but sideways forces develop (see Fig 5.3). Forces acting at the top of the mast can exert considerable leverage on the hull and in high wind speeds cause the boat to roll and can lead to the infamous 'Death Roll' leeward broach. So have one of the crew keep the top batten trimmed correctly, even in light to medium airs when the differential in performance will be greatest. Without a rigid vang in light airs the weight of the boom can cause the leech to close up, so use a spare halyard to lift the end of the boom slightly to open it up again.

Heavy airs techniques

Running in heavy airs sometimes calls for more aggressive trimming on the main. The latest IMS hull shapes are certainly fast downwind and in surfing conditions boatspeed and apparent wind angle can change dramatically in seconds. Big wide sterns and narrow rudders can make it difficult for helmsmen to regain control if the boat starts to broach out to one side or another. Sailing an IMS 40 footer in such conditions with a mainsheet track that stretched the width of the boat, I found it faster to haul in the traveller to windward to stop each roll developing, rather than trying to tension the vang or wind in the mainsheet winch. Use whatever control on your boat allows you to pull the mainsail in as fast as possible and then to be able to let it out just as fast. A rapid response to the first hint of a roll is the best way to prevent the problem. It can be helped by the spinnaker being flown further to leeward than usual with the pole low and tweaker line down hard to stabilise and deepen the base of the sail and to encourage the kite shoulders to flatten out. As a rule try to keep the centre seam of the spinnaker lined up with the fore stay by moving the guy and sheet in tandem, so keeping the centre of effort over the centreline.

The technique most inexperienced helmsmen initially find hard to grasp is curtailing the rolling by steering the boat underneath the rig. As soon as the centre of effort of the sail plan moves away from being directly above the centre of resistance of the hull and foils, then the rig will roll in that direction. To prevent the ensuing broach and to get the boat upright again, turn the rudder abruptly to get the hull back under the rig. So long as this sudden turn is corrected quickly, it does not matter if the yacht is by-the-lee for a second. You will soon get a feel for how far you can throw the boat around without broaching to windward or chinese gybing. It is just like trying to balance a pencil on your finger tip.

Masthead yachts can have more of a problem in these conditions as there is a lot more unstable nylon flying around up high, which is hard to control. A small narrow shouldered chute is the answer for heavy airs; but make sure it is cut flat in the top. Racing an IMX 38 (masthead rig) in a windy winter series race one year the owner brought along a 1.5 oz kite from his previous fractional 38 footer which had been re-cut with extra cross panels to make up the luff length. As we headed down the run in a gusty 25 knots with another IMX 38 some 10–12 lengths astern, a conservative call went out for the 'Chicken Chute'. WIth the 1.5 oz doctored kite flying the boat was rolling around more than it should have been with a small sail and I, on the main, was having to use the full length of the track to counter each oscillation. What was happening was that the altered spinnaker, not being designed for the job, had ended up with tight round leeches, adding considerable depth to the head. The top of the sail could not readily exhaust and was rocking around at the top of the mast, rolling the boat underneath it. Our rivals behind with a full size 0.75 oz were steadily gaining whilst our boat lurched precariously downwind. Just before the mark a gust caught the helmsman steering a little too low, the unstable kite rolled the boat to windward, I pulled the traveller all the way up to the stop expecting the boat to roll back but this time it did not. I then realised I was up to my chest in water! Do not kid yourself that the boat will be more controllable with a smaller spinnaker up. Being able to flatten off and open up the top of the sail is far more important.

Steering downwind

Tiller steering the modern race boat can be hard work if the rudder is small, so do not be embarrassed to ask for help. Have a co-pilot sit opposite you with his hands resting on the tiller to help out when it gets heavy.

The last thing a helmsman needs is too much windward helm, so the mainsheet trimmer must always be ready to dump the main completely to prevent the boat from rounding up. The mainsail should always be released first, before the spinnaker, as keeping the power on at the front will help the helmsman to bear off. If a broach does occur do not try to fight it by keeping the rudder hard over as it will never work whilst stalled out. Centre the helm to re-establish attached flow or try pumping it hard a couple of times if it fails to respond.

The technique, once committed to a broach, is to steer into it in an effort to keep the boat moving. Let the sails fly and keep the crew weight on the rail until the boat comes upright. If the boat still has some way on it will respond more quickly to the helm. So accept the fact that a broach is inevitable and focus on trying to keep the rudder working and some speed on the boat, so that as soon as the boat comes up you have sufficient steerage to bear off and avoid a repeat performance.

When the right wind and sea directions combine to create possible surfing conditions, the helmsman needs to work closely with the trimmers to try to catch the free ride offered by the passing waves. Waves tend to come in sets of three, with the third one being bigger than the rest. Head up across the face of the smaller waves to build speed and await the big one that lifts the stern more than the norm. Up by the mast the spinnaker trimmer waits for the bow to dip lower than usual. Whoever spots a good wave first shouts, 'Wave', or 'Now.' and the helmsman bears off perhaps 10–20° down the back of it and at the same instant both the main and kite trimmer pump the sheet (but no more than once, see IYRU rule 54.3(b)) to help lift the bow and help stay on the wave. Catch one right and stay with it a few seconds and you can pull out a boatlength or so on the opposition – great for breaking or creating an overlap on the approach to the gybe mark.

Catching a tow

It was proved to me last Cowes Week just how effective gaining a tow offwind from a larger yacht can be, whilst I was racing a One Tonner with a wily old master of the art, John McWilliam. John actually put the CHS rating of the boat up by increasing the cross widths of an old spinnaker so that the boat rated as the lowest in Class 1. The thinking behind this was that the only trophies worth winning were in Class 1, and in light airs a small boat will usually do well. Cowes Week being the first week of August, the chances of a few light days was well worth the gamble. All we had to do was stick close to the main opposition, a well sailed Swan 46. Upwind we were usually ahead of *Crackajack* and several other bigger Cruiser racers, but they soon caught up downwind. As one approached from astern we 'soaked down' to their line, and as they passed the helmsman was instructed to drop on to the first stern wave, about half a length to windward and astern. The trimmers then had to work like crazy to stay there and suddenly we were running 2/10ths of a knot faster, being sucked along by the bigger boat. A slip on the helm or hole in the breeze and the boat would drop us off the first wave and on to the second or third which was slower and harder to stay on, yet still added to the speed. To get a tow you need the wind angle, wind strength and waves to be just right, but on a long run offshore it can be the perfect way to save your time on handicap. *Sidewinder*, our mount, ended the week with two of the big trophies and two seconds, much to the resentment of the rest of the fleet who were fed up with watching the smallest boat in the class glued to their stern!

VMG, Target Speed and Polar Diagrams Explained

Despite all the fancy jargon, target speed, VMG and polars are in fact quite simple concepts once examined.

Target speed is the speed the boat should be going to achieve maximum velocity made good. VMG is best explained by Fig 5.A and upwind VMG can be described as the velocity made good towards the wind. Put simply, VMG is a measure of the yacht's progress directly to windward. It helps you decide if it is better to sail free (and therefore faster) but further to get to the windward mark or to sail as high as you can and sail less distance but more slowly. The optimum route will provide the highest value of VMG. The answer changes with each variation in wind speed, so how do you know what speed and angle the boat should be attaining upwind?

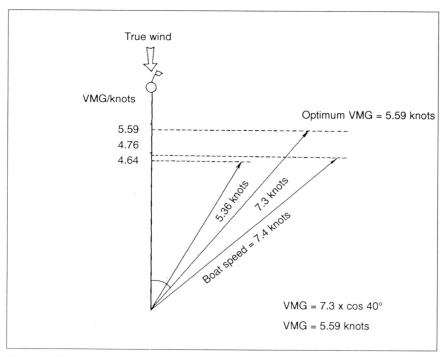

Fig 5.A *VMG helps to find the optimum speed to windward.*

Downwind VMG is a similar concept but is a measure of the fastest way to get dead downwind. Here there are many more combinations of speeds and angles to sail, depending upon the wind speed and angle. In both cases the general rule is that the higher the wind speed, the closer it is possible to sail to the wind or rhumbline.

In answer to the question of what is the correct speed and heading to sail to achieve the optimum VMG for a certain wind speed, we turn to the notion of a 'target speed'. It is possible to fit an instrument which provides a constant readout of VMG, but I find the use of target speeds is better. Attempting to maximise a VMG readout can in fact be slow, as it is a function of the VMG measurement that the velocity values will shoot up the nearer you sail to the wind. Thus if the helmsman mindlessly follows the VMG instrument, you would end up sailing too close to the wind, at which stage the boat would suddenly stall out and stop, boatspeed would crash, and so in turn would VMG.

Target speed is a more healthy way of reaching a good, steady VMG, as it provides a speed to aim at, for a given wind speed. Not only does it make the crew work hard to hit the target speed but you also have the satisfaction of knowing the boat is sailing at maximum VMG. When boatspeed exceeds the target speed, it means that the helmsman is sailing too low and fast, and is therefore sailing at a lower angle than that of the optimum VMG. So head up and trade a little speed for height. On the other hand,

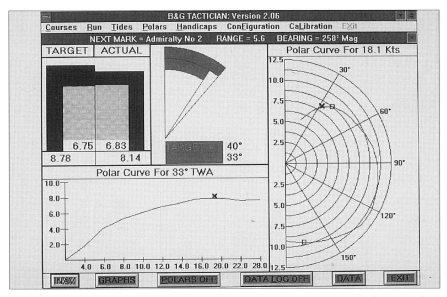

The position on the curve where optimum VMG both up and downwind is marked by squares. Photo: *Brookes and Gatehouse Ltd*

one reason for not managing to hit the target speed could be that the boat is heading too high upwind and should bear off and sail a little faster (or 'fatter' as American sailors would say) or if downwind, is sailing too low and should head up to go faster.

Upwind it is simpler to have a list of target speeds written up in the cockpit, in the view of the helmsman, so that he can see at a glance the target speed for every two knots of true wind speed. Downwind you could be reaching all over the ocean, trying to find the correct angle to provide the target speed, so a true wind angle is generally provided next to the target speed angle. But where does all this information come from? Enter the polar diagram. The polar diagram is at first glance a complex picture of concentric circles, but it is really just a simple graph with three rather than two axes. Each ring is a plot of boat speed for a particular wind strength and each point on the curve corresponds to a wind strength value. Only

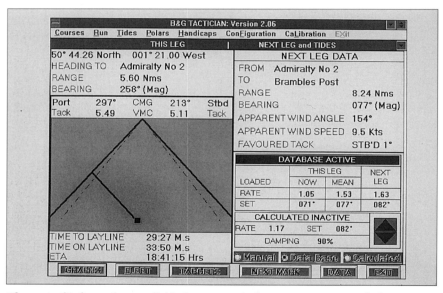

The sort of information available from a tactical racing program, including course and bearing to the next mark, and time and distance to the laylines. Photo: *Brookes and Gatehouse Ltd.*

half the diagram is drawn usually, as the curves are always symmetrical. The other half of the diagram would show the same information, but on the other tack or gybe. (See Photo on page 81).

A polar diagram is generated specifically for each design of boat or one-design class and can be produced from the yacht designer's computer design program or from the measurements collected for an IMS measurement certificate. Any boat that has an IMS certificate can obtain a polar diagram for a small charge from their national rating office. (The RORC

Rating office in Lymington in the UK, or the USYRU in Newport, Rhode Island in the USA.) However, the most accurate polar diagram is likely to come from the yacht's original design program, simply because it is likely to be several generations ahead of the original MIT velocity prediction program which lies at the heart of the IMS system. Almost every new race boat is today delivered with a set of 'polars' to help the crew get the boat up to speed as soon as the boat hits the water.

The degree to which the information provided by the polars is used is up to you. There are several ways of utilising the data depending upon the level of the campaign. Round the cans racer cruiser sailors may have a waterproof copy of the diagram aboard with the core numbers written up in the cockpit, as an aid to the afterguard when selecting downwind angles on a free leg of the course and for the trimmers to check their target speeds upwind.

These days, Grand Prix boats are more likely to carry onboard computer which is integrated to all of the yacht's instruments. This allows the navigator/tactician to sit on the rail with a waterproof lap top PC on his knees and have constant access to a whole range of real time information. Not only the basics of boatspeed, speed over the ground, course over the ground, true wind angle, but also computed data of the difference between target speed and actual speed, plots of true wind speed and direction and tidal flow. When linked to a GPS, then course and distance to the next mark, time to the layline etc can all be displayed on screen. Some of these software packages can also record the boat's progress throughout the race,

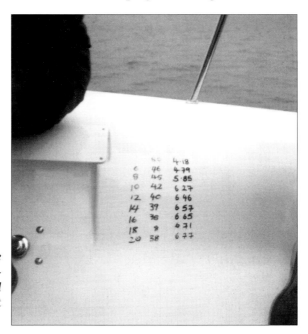

Target speeds can be taken from a polar diagram and displayed somewhere in the cockpit for easy reference.

allowing the crew to 're-run' the race later ashore to compare target speeds and optimum VMG to those actually achieved and to see when and why the boat was slow. Was it due to a poor headsail choice, or was the helmsman off form at a particular stage? Such technology can also be used to assess and compare sails and to help define their optimum wind range. The software can automatically; update the stored polar information as a predicted target speed is bettered, allowing the polars to be 'fine tuned' to the individual boat and the performance of its sails.

There is already talk of incorporating radar systems into the PC, so that the speed and track of other yachts could be monitored on screen, so for instance the tactician could tell if he was going to cross a starboard tracker in 10 minutes time and if the boats on the other side of the course were gaining or losing. Where will it all end!

But before investing in the latest tactical racing PC system, ensure you have a technical and PC literate tactician aboard, who can fully understand and utilise both the soft and hardware. As all the computer experts will tell you, 'garbage in = garbage out,' so all the boat's instruments need to be religiously calibrated. Tactical software programs should be used as an additional tool to aid the tactician/navigator's acquired skills and experience and not to replace them.

Part 2: TACTICS

6. *Starting Tactics and the Upwind Leg*

Every book on yacht racing will tell you how crucial the start can be and how races are often won or lost from the very beginning. We all know this, but why is it that the techniques and skills involved in starting are rarely practised or explained? Crews can spend hours practising gybing or refining boatspeed, yet the single most important element of winning a yacht race is left to one attempt on race day. The reason is that to practise starting effectively you need a proper laid line, other boats on it and someone to run the starting sequence – not an exercise a crew can easily organise on its own. The best form of practice is therefore lots of short, sharp races with a single beat and run.

Starting in the right place and going the correct way in the opening minutes of a race used to be a complete mystery to me before I learnt how to work out which end of the line was favoured, and – more importantly – the order of priority in starting. By this I mean working out which is the most important *factor* at the start. For example, there is little point in starting right at the leeward end to take advantage of a 100 line bias if there is a major tidal advantage or a persistent shift out on the righthand side of the course which you cannot get to because your boat is trapped on the left. During my early days of dinghy racing I used to quiz the race winner as to why he started at a particular end and what made him choose his route up the first beat. When the answers begin to coincide with your own assessment of the situation, your confidence starts to build and the mystery begins to unravel.

For the regatta sailor there are five main starting techniques which need to be learnt and understood before he or she can consistently pull off a good start:

1 Calculating the extent and direction of any line bias.
2 Deciding which end to start, taking into account line bias, tidal strength, and angle and direction of likely wind shifts.
3 Selecting a transit to ensure you know exactly where the line is.
4 Positioning your boat on the line, and creating and protecting a space to leeward.

5 Time on distance judgement, so that the boat accelerates at the right time to hit the line at full speed.

Pre-start routine

At a couple of regattas I have been nearly caught out by the Race Officer setting up his line and beginning the starting sequence very quickly, with the pin end buoy going down after the 10 minute gun. (It must be in place before the 5 minute signal.) Be aware that some Race Officers like to start on time and the fact that most of the fleet are tuning their boats halfway up the beat will not deter them from beginning the starting procedure.

Aim to arrive at the starting area at least an hour before the start. Immediately sail upwind, set the boat up for the expected conditions, track the wind by noting its bearing every five minutes and monitor the tide at any marks. It is worth sailing out to both extremes of the beat to see if there is any marked difference in the wind direction or strength. Is there a wind bend as you sail in towards the cliffs? Are you headed as you sail out to sea, and is it sunny enough for a sea breeze to fill in? As you run back down to the start with half an hour to go, the crew should be discussing what they have found and making a decision as to which way to go up the first beat, irrespective at this stage of any line bias.

With the boat carefully aligned on the start line, take the bearing of the line from the bow using a central compass.

Take a transit to any landmark on the shore. Stand up as high as you can to obtain a clear view.

A typical conversation might be: 'Well it looks like a sea breeze may come in, the sky's clear, it is getting hot and it was forecast. Do we want to head for the right?' 'Yes, but there will be less tide against us on the left. Which is more important?' 'Hopefully most the fleet will know about the tide and will want to take a long tack in to the shore. If we start to windward of the fleet and go towards the left we will be on the right side of the fleet if the breeze flicks to the right and we should get more wind there too.' 'OK, let's go and see what the line looks like.'

With your race plan beginning to take shape get back to the line before all the others boats do, so that you can get a clear bearing on the line and pick a transit with a distinctive feature on the shore if possible. The best place to sight a transit is from right by the committee boat. Using the engine, position the boat exactly; on the extension of the start line to allow the bowman to get a good feel for where the line is and to choose a transit. The tactician can also use this moment to take a bearing down the line with a hand-bearing compass. Everyone else will probably have the same idea, so hang around close to the committee boat so that as soon as the line is down you can be the first on to it to measure the angle. If under engine, it is relatively easy to position the boat exactly on the line by alignment of the fore stay with the pin buoy and the back stay with the mast on the committee boat, whilst sighting the compass on the centreline.

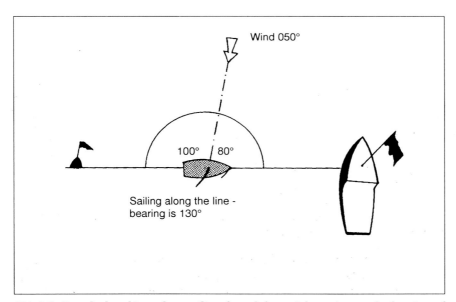

Fig 6.1 *To calculate bias when sailing from left to right, subtract the bearing of the wind (50°) from that of the line (130°). 130° − 50° = 80°. If more than 90° the left side is favoured. If 90° exactly, the line is square.*

Calculating the bias

A competent Race Officer will tend to set a start line with a 5°–10° port tack bias, in order to encourage the fleet to spread out along the line. If there is a good reason for going right up the beat, such as a big tidal benefit, the port end bias may be more, to tempt yachts away from the piling up at the committee boat end and making life difficult for the Race Officer.

More occasionally there may be a starboard end bias if the lefthand side of the course is heavily favoured. However, in a shifty breeze the bias can frequently change and may not end up as the Race Officer intended.

To my mind, it is vital to know how much bias there is on the start line. The only way to measure it is to take a bearing along the line, then measure the wind angle, add 90° to that and see if it is more or less than the bearing of the line (see Fig 6.1). All the other methods you will read about in textbooks, such as reaching down the line with the main cleated etc, will tell you which is the favoured end, but they will not tell you by how much. The reason you need to measure the amount of bias is because your starting position on the line depends to a great extend on the *degree* of bias.

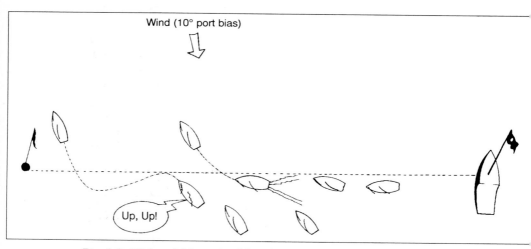

Fig 6.2 *With a 10° port end bias and the left side of the beat favoured, aim to start a third up from the pin end.*

If there is only 5° it would be good to start a third up from the favoured end, but if you wanted to go up the opposite side for the beat for any reason, forget the bias and start at the other end in order to take that side of the course. When a line has 10° of bias you have to start taking it seriously and position the boat towards that end. Starting a third up from the pin is usually favourite as you miss the scrum right at the mark (some boats invariably misjudge it and get there too early). If the situation is as our crew found before the race where there is a 10° port end bias but the sea breeze could swing the wind to the right, start towards the port end but to the right of the majority of the fleet, so leaving your options open to tack to the right if the wind shifts.

Occasionally you will come across a line with a bias of 15°–20° or more, either due to a major wind shift just before the start or an inept Race Officer! In this case whichever boat starts right at the favoured end will be among the leaders around the windward mark. With this amount of bias there is only one place to start.

Starting techniques

Situation 1:   10° port end bias, left side of the beat is favoured, 10 knots true wind.

In this case the aim is to start a third up from the pin, create a gap immediately to leeward in which to bear off into to accelerate just before the start (see Fig 6.2). With 1½ to 2 minutes to go, sail up the line from the leeward end towards the fleet, the majority of whom will be reaching down on starboard. Tack just before they reach you and luff slowly so that the bow is just on the line. The transit you took earlier is vital now to tell you exactly where the line is.

There are now 50 seconds to the start. The bow is pointing 10° off the wind, the sails are well eased out and flapping. The rest of the fleet is now reaching down at you with alarming speed. The tactician (ideally not the helmsman who should be concentrating 100 per cent on his position and timing) starts to shout at the rapidly approaching boats, 'Up, up, keep clear,' as loudly as possible. If the other crews are proficient sailors they should abide by your call and slow or luff their boats to keep clear to windward. (Remember IYRR 38.2 requires any luff before the start to be slow and to allow the boat to windward room and opportunity to keep clear.)

With your boat now parked right on the line, the fleet to windward will all be having to slow down and stack-up above you, or will have to bear off and duck the boats to leeward. The remainder of the fleet to the left will carry on reaching down the line for the pin, leaving a gap to leeward. If there are other boats close by to leeward trying the same thing, you must hold your boat still on the line until they sail away down the line, without letting any of those above you sail over the top. The key is to be patient here and wait for the leeward boat to put its bow down and sheet in.

Now, depending on the wind strength, the helmsman and tactician have to choose the moment to bear off into the gap that has just been created to leeward, allowing enough time for the boat to accelerate to full hull speed before the gun. In 10 knots of wind in a 30 foot race boat this could take between 15 and 20 seconds but in a heavy cruiser racer it could be 30 to 45 seconds. If there is a large gap to leeward and no danger of arriv-

This start at the Commodore's Cup shows how the leeward boat on the right, luffing almost head to wind on the line, is preventing the boats to windward from sailing over the top of her. The windward boat's only choice is to bear off below the luffing yacht or be forced over the line early. The leeward yacht has then successfully defended her space and thus has room in which to bear off and gather speed seconds before the gun.

ing at the pin too soon, you obviously have more time and room to build up speed. The larger the fleet and the shorter the line the harder it is to create the gap, but if you do not have room to build the necessary speed the fleet will simply reach over your boat and leave you standing and wondering where it all went wrong. If your boat is one of the smaller yachts in the fleet be aware of larger boats coming up fast from below trying to force a gap; so have someone keep lookout astern.

The helmsman and tactician need to sort out between themselves who is going to call the shots during the pre-start. One may be more experienced than the other at big fleet starts and it can work well if the helmsman has complete faith in his tactician and does exactly as he is instructed. This frees the tactician to move around the boat checking the situation to leeward and astern, whilst the helmsman concentrates on where he is going and controlling the speed of the boat. Other helmsmen prefer some input from the tactician about other boats around, but choose the positioning on the line and judge the timing themselves.

The vital skills here that the rest of the crew need to develop are holding the boat on station without sliding to leeward and so losing the hard fought gap and time on distance judgement, so that you do not accelerate only to arrive at the pin still with 10 seconds to go. The problem many mid-fleet sailors encounter when trying to stop the boat dead on the line is that they let the sails right out but keep the bow down and end up sailing into the gap they have just created. The technique is to turn the boat sharply into the wind, push the boom out hard to stop going over the line and even sail backwards if necessary. However, once stopped, return the bow to 10° off the wind with the sails out over the quarter flapping. If you keep the bow into the wind there is a big danger of getting stuck head to wind precisely at the moment when you need to sheet in and get moving.

Despite positioning your boat perfectly for the start, there will always be those around you who either do not know exactly where the line is or get excited and start pushing over the line too soon. Once another boat sails over the top of you and interferes with your wind it is all too late. The only way to avoid a premature starter ruining your start is never to let them get there in the first place. Enthusiastic and slightly aggressive shouting can deter the cowboy starter from getting too close to you in the last few seconds but if he is determined to start early there is not much you can do. Be careful that your cries of 'Up, up' etc do not force the other boat over the line into your path. Rather try to psyche the opposition into not daring to sail over your boat.

If yachts on both sides start to go early and their sails are hiding you from the eagle eyed Race Officer, then you should keep level with them and go forward with the pack. The chances are that it will be a general recall, but if it is not and you are left three lengths back, but on the right side of the line, that top ten position at the windward mark will be out of reach. But, do make sure you are hidden if you decide to go early. The occasion to sit back and let the cowboys go is when the black flag is flying. Having lost a third place at a national championship I now start much more conservatively under the sudden death rule!

Situation 2:   15° port end bias, 6 knots true wind, 1.5 knots of foul tide
In this case, taken from the Dragon Edinburgh Cup at Lowestoft a few years ago, it was vital to take the bias and start under the committee boat, as the light breeze was likely to shift to the right. However, with a 45 foot committee boat, little wind and a sluicing tide, sailing up inside the start boat was impossible. The most important point in a light airs start is to keep speed on the boat the whole time and come in to the line later than the rest with maximum speed, and cruise over the top of the slowing boats which arrive too early. With so much tide we had to keep above the line, and decided to duck down at the last minute from this position, picking up full speed to hit the line at the gun. The other big benefit of starting near one end or the other in light airs and a foul tide is that it is a lot easier to judge the line accurately and it is less distance to sail round the ends if caught over the line early (see Fig 6.3).

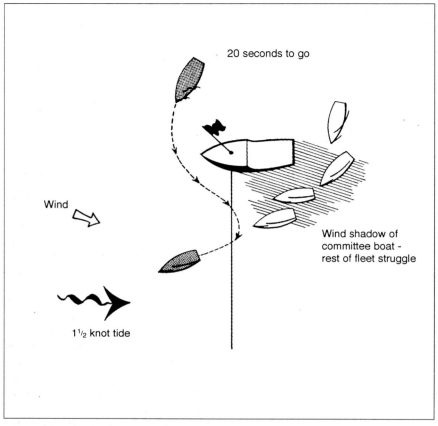

20 seconds to go

Wind

Wind shadow of
committee boat -
rest of fleet struggle

1½ knot tide

Fig 6.3 *In light airs and against a foul tide, starting from above the committee boat can be a good trick.*

So with 20 seconds to go we bore off from above the committee boat, ducked the line, sheeted in and crossed the line at full speed. After 10 seconds I looked back to see a pack of boats crawling around the back of the committee boat, with no speed, yet to cross the line. To prove it is such an advantage to have a great start in such conditions, we rounded the mark 3rd and went on to win the race.

At the gun

Many sailors think that the thing to do as the gun goes is to sheet in hard and try to sail as high as possible. I used to do this and wondered why the boats either side would soon sail over the top and leave me sitting in the whole fleet's dirty air. In fact you should sail low out of the start, down into the space you previously created to leeward, in order to build speed as quickly as possible. As the boat reaches hull speed the keel and rudder become more efficient in generating lift and so it is much easier to then gain height to windward. Obviously height is important after the start, but do not try to point high too soon. Conversely you cannot afford to bear off underneath another boat, and if someone does start too close to leeward you will struggle to keep above them after the gun.

There will always be bad starts when, for some reason, you do not get away in the front rank and in clear air. When it happens you must instantly look to see the earliest opportunity to tack off under the fleet to find clear air. The sooner you can tack the less you will lose, even if it means dipping many transoms.

There are of course many different methods of starting, the choice of which will be dictated by the priorities of each situation. Some helmsmen like making a pin end start by using a timed run from the committee boat, others in a shifting breeze will sit in the middle of the line until two minutes to go, then choose the favoured end and sail towards it.

Once you have learned to prioritise the most important factors of a start, your choice of where and how to make that start will rapidly improve. The confidence and satisfaction to be gained from getting it right is the ideal boost to help get the boat around that windward mark first.

Tactics after the start

At a Dragon Gold Cup in Scotland one year we pulled off what I thought was a pretty smart start. Having figured out there was around 12° of bias at the pin end buoy and that the wind was persistently going left, we hit the line four lengths up from the buoy as the gun fired. As we came away from the line the breeze began to head and we started to look good. There was just one boat to leeward, which was Poul Richard Hoj Jensen of Denmark. The knock held as we sailed towards the lefthand side of the course, carrying the Danish boat with us. Working on the dangerous principle that 'if a little is good, more must be better', I decided to hold on further to the left. Eventually we tacked and rounded somewhere in the first six. Ashore after the race I spoke to Poul Richard about the great first leg. I was surprised to find the genial Dane a little less than happy. 'After a start like that you should have crossed the fleet,' he explained. 'If you ever see you have the chance to cross you must go straight away. He was evidently not pleased that we had held him on all the way to the left side of the course. If the breeze had flicked back to the right we would have looked pretty stupid, having previously been clear ahead on the left, not to have 'banked' our advantage by tacking back to cover the fleet. I always remember that lesson from the double Olympic gold medallist: never be greedy! The upwind leg is like a game of chess. Make your move, consolidate the gain and then work on your next move.

Throughout the first half of the beat, the tactician needs to spend all his time working out exactly what is happening on the race course, whilst the rest of the crew quietly concentrate on sailing the boat as fast as possible. It is impossible to plan your strategy if you do not have an overall picture in your mind of which way the wind is moving and what is happening to your boat in relation to the rest of the fleet.

The tactician gleans the information he requires from three distinct sources:

1 **The yacht's instrumentation.** Principally compass heading, speed, course over the ground (COG), speed over the ground (SOG) and position (from the GPS or Decca). From these data the tactician can quickly ascertain boatspeed, if the boat has been lifted or headed since the start, if the tide is with or against and by how much, and what the exact position is in relation to the next mark.

2 **The relative position of the main competition.** By keeping track of the progress of the yachts on either extremes of the course, either visually or by bearing using a hand-held compass, the tactician can decide which side of the beat is paying. If there is a persistent lift on starboard tack, then all the boats to windward on the same tack will gain. If there is no wind shift evident on your boat but all the boats inshore are gaining, then it may be due to them being in less foul tide or more wind. The tell-tale signs to watch for when monitoring boats away off in the distance are:
   • *Angle of heel*, indicating the amount of wind the boat is currently experiencing. (Don't be fooled by the modern breed of IMS racers, though, many of which have incredibly high righting moments and so appear upright in the water whilst older designs will be exhibiting a greater degree of heel.)
   • *Relative heading.* Is the other boat on a parallel course to yours or sailing closer to the wind, or have they been headed off? Some crews use terms like, 'They look bow down over there,' meaning 'that boat appears to be headed, as the bow is angled further off the wind.' 'Bow up,' or 'Stern down,' means the opposite.

3 **Current meteorological conditions and weather forecast.** The tactician should have available a detailed local forecast covering the duration of the race, either from an onboard weather fax or collected by phone or fax before the start. A basic knowledge of meteorology helps to spot impending changes in the breeze, such as an approaching front (cumulus cloud stacking downwards), a developing sea breeze (air becomes colder), dramatic wind shifts (big black clouds), and numerous other signs.

Once the tactician has built up a picture of the way the wind is moving, he or she can decide upon a mean wind angle. Once the breeze shifts below this mean angle, it is time to look for a tack. Alternatively if the wind takes you higher than the mean value, indicating a good lift, stay on the good heading if possible until it shifts back. When a suitable shift back below the mean arrives, sail into it to check it is not just a short-lived pulse in velocity before deciding to tack.

Wind shifts are not, however, the only factors to determine when to tack. The tactician has to work out the implications of every tack before committing to it and consider all the possible 'what if' scenarios. The other vital factors to bear in mind when considering a tack are: maintaining clear air (would a tack now place you in the dirty air of another yacht?), keeping a cover on the opposition astern, or trying to break cover if being covered yourself. Other tactical implications also come into play, such as getting to a certain side of the course for tidal reasons or, in the case of a persistent lift, working your way to that side to be on the inside of the lift. In big one-design fleets just avoiding the traffic can be a nightmare, but it does help a lot if you are out in front!

If the wind is swinging wildly and there is no tidal variation across the course, the safest option is to go up the middle. You may make only small gains but more importantly your losses will only be small too. The tactician also has to decide when to attack and when to defend and protect the boat's current position. His decisions will be different for each situation but will always come down to his skill, experience and knowledge of the boat.

Covering the opposition

There are several types of cover, each suitable for a particular stage in the race. On the first upwind leg, assuming a good position within the top ten, you should employ a loose cover on the major opposition. If most of your rivals hit the left hard but you feel there is a stronger breeze on the right, it would be folly to leave them to it. By the second beat the order will be better established, making it evident which boats to cover. You cannot hope to cover both sides of the course, so choose what you believe to be the most beneficial route to the next mark and loosely cover the opposition that follows the same way. If your boatspeed is good, you do not need to cover the bulk of the fleet, only those boats fast enough to pose a threat. Near the top of the beat you may be able to take a more middle track to keep an eye on both sides of the course.

Sailing with Poul Richard Hoj Jensen when he won the Dragon Gold Cup in 1992, I was surprised how far he would let the opposition get away upwind. The wind conditions off Ostend that week were typically a steady 10–16 knots with small 5° shifts due to pulses in the wind velocity. As the opposition was often spread across both wings of the course, our track was more often towards the middle but keeping a good eye on boats either side. Once it became evident that a group were gaining out to sea we made no great dash to get over there. Probably by the time we got there, the small shift would have gone back and we would have had to follow the rest into the mark. Instead Poul Richard concentrated hard on boatspeed at the top of the beat and keeping the boat flat, to ensure crossing ahead of the boats coming across from out to sea. Approaching the mark in this way gave us the choice of tacking on the small but crucial shifts; whilst those boats coming in on the layline did not have that option.

During the middle stages of a race, a situation can often arise where you are just ahead of a rival yacht, but do not wish to slap a tight cover on them quite yet. To do so would only force them to tack off, and in doing so you may hand over control because, with you committed to covering, they then make the decision when to tack. If, instead, you tack into a loose covering position ahead but to leeward, you do not force the other boat to tack. By not threatening your rival, you can keep contact with them whilst you sail towards the side of the course you wish to take. For instance, if a third boat was getting away on the far side and was likely to find a favourable shift, it would be wise to cover. If the second boat was heading that way, by tacking to leeward you can shepherd them in the right direction, and so end up herding the opposition the way you wish to go, at the same time staying ahead.

The golden rule for covering on the last upwind leg is always to stay between the opposition and the finish. If two boats come around the bottom mark close together and one tacks off in the opposite direction, you should ordinarily choose the nearest one to cover. That is, unless you have to beat the third boat to win the series or, when handicap racing, if the third boat carries a lower TCF (time correction factor) and is hence more of a threat. If your boat is being closely covered and there is no danger from behind then attack the boat ahead with a tacking duel. Tack immediately at the mark so that the covering yacht is forced into the disturbed air of the remainder of the fleet running in to the mark. Keep tacking to slow the other boat down. Your tacks should be quicker since you choose when to go whereas the covering boat has to keep their eyes glued on you and tack in response.

If the covering is so tight that the other boat puts the helm over the instant your helmsman does, you can try selling them a dummy tack. Once they have slapped a few tacks right on top of you and are feeling pretty confident, make sure they are watching you when the cockpit crew set up for the next tack. Quietly pass the word to the crew that you are going for a dummy tack. Slowly initiate the tack so that the headsail is released and the boom comes into the middle of the boat and then look to see if the covering boat follows. Once they are committed to the tack, jerk the helm back to fall back on to the old tack and watch the other boat sail off into the distance. If you fail, don't try the same trick again, as this time they will be watching for it. Other moves to 'wipe off' the covering boat include timing your tack to put the covering yacht nicely in the wind shadow of another boat ahead or splitting the tacks with boat astern so that the covering boat is torn between which one to go with.

Maintaining a tight cover in this way should prevent any boat of similar speed getting through, as the boats will be close enough to experience the same wind conditions. If your cover is sufficiently tight they should not be able to sail through your dirty air.

Approaching the windward mark

Avoid hitting the layline too early as other boats will simply tack on top, slow you dramatically and in foul tide there is a danger your boat may no longer be able to fetch the buoy. Aim to make your attack at around four boatlengths by choosing the moment to tack into an overlap position. At this close proximity to the mark it makes judging the tack a lot simpler and gives the opposition less time to react to your presence; either by bearing down on you or trying to establish a last minute overlap inside.

On the occasions when the tide is under you, tack slightly below the mark and luff if necessary to get round, rather than searching for a gap in the queue above the layline. Figure 6.4 shows how easy it is to overstand the mark when tacking into a gap in the line of boats on the layline. Each port tacker coming in to the mark has to sail a little further than the boat he crosses behind in order to gain clear air and avoid being slowed.

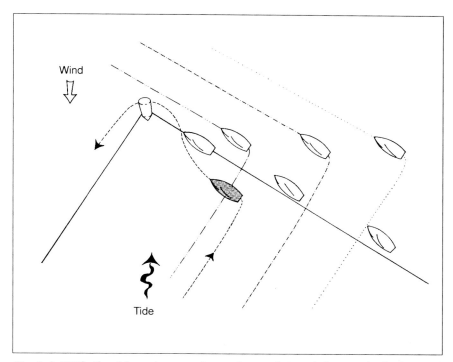

Fig 6.4 *With the tide under you, boats that tack into holes on the layline end up being pushed beyond the layline to the windward mark.*

Coming in late on port requires a steady nerve but it saves sailing a lot of extra distance.

A good tactician will be able to judge which yacht will make the mark first and how much room you will have at the buoy. He should also have at the back of his mind an alternative way out if the original plan does not come off.

Big fleet one-design racing teaches you to develop conservative tactics. In the opening races of a 60 plus fleet regatta, identify the likely top boats and aim to roughly stay with them up the first few beats so that your results will not be far off theirs. Hopefully, with a few safe but solid top ten results under your belt the tactician then has more scope for more radical and slightly more risky tactics in the remaining races.

7. Tactics Offwind and at the Finish

One thing you soon learn in a big one-design keelboat fleet is how easy it can be to lose a lot of places on the reach. All the boats tend to go at much the same speed across the wind but if the boat behind makes a better mark rounding and manages to break through to windward throwing you disturbed air, in a matter of seconds a whole pack of boats close astern can be through.

Once around the mark, be it the windward or a gybe mark, your first priority in a close fleet is usually to claim and then protect the windward berth. Sail high out of the mark to dissuade those behind from trying to climb above. If you arrive at the gybe mark with a lot of other boats it is vital to do a quick, tight gybe, bang the pole forward to the fore stay, hike like crazy, and reach up to windward of the pack to protect your air. One top Danish Soling sailor used to use a twinning line with a hook on the end instead of a block, so that just before the gybe mark this hook could be clipped on to the clew of the spinnaker. The twinning line was just long enough to reach the fore stay and the idea was that as the pole came of the mast and the boat gybed, the helmsman could luff the boat hard to get to windward, the twinning line would hold the spinnaker at the fore stay in a close reaching position and the fore deck crew could then clip the pole on to what had now become a lazy guy without having a huge load on the guy to work against.

Further down the reach when you have settled on the course to the next mark, you need all the warning possible in order to respond to a luff from astern. Have someone sitting at the back of the boat keep his eyes trained on the pursuing pack, watching for the tell-tale signs of an impending strike, such as the pole going forward, the mainsheet coming in or weight being transferred to the windward side. If they do make a move, drop the pole on to the fore stay and show you are fully prepared to luff them to kingdom come if they dare to try to come past!

When to sail low on the reach

If the boat does get rolled but you are then able to clear your air quickly by luffing up, then do so if you feel you can then maintain the windward berth. If, however, there is still a wall of sailcloth to windward or a number of larger yachts steaming up astern, the tactician may decide that it would be better to sail low and avoid the dirty air above.

The common fault many helmsmen make is, having sailed low and gained places on the first two-thirds of the leg, they then reach up to windward too early. At the critical few lengths before the mark they once again come under the windshadow of the rest of the fleet and lose all the previous hard fought gain. Try to remember that a place gain offwind does not count until you 'bank' it by passing ahead at the next mark.

In a mixed fleet, if your boat is at the smaller end of the class and you arrive at the turning mark up amongst the big boys, it may pay to bear off low to avoid the worst of the eventual dirty air (tidal conditions permitting). Similarly, if you suffer a bad first beat in a handicap class or end up at the back of a large one-design fleet, it is often quicker to sail around the smaller and slower opposition than through them. Tail-end-Charlies, surprised to find a top boat behind them, can suddenly come to life, become ultra competitive and delight in luffing or tacking right on top of unfortunate 'Rock Stars'. Other occasions when it pays to sail low on the reach are:

- When a boat is forced to round the mark on the outside of a group of yachts and is then pinned to lee of the bunch.
- If there is a significant tidal stream flowing in the opposite direction to the wind.

When the tide is carrying the boat up to windward, you obviously have to sail on a heading below the mark to avoid overstanding. However, in a shifting breeze beware of cracking off and sailing low too early, only to have the wind head, and end up beating back up to the buoy. If the tide is running the opposite way, pushing you off the mark, it is safer to sail a little too high than get caught low, since doing so will also help to protect your wind. On long reaching legs, use a GPS with a graphic display of the track and cross track error to check that you are not sailing too far from the tide corrected rhumb line.

I learnt how to sail low to avoid 'dirty air' from watching a German Dragon sailor, Markus Glas, at the 1987 Europeans in Helsinki. On several occasions Glas was down around mid-fleet and forced to round the mark on the outside. He clearly had good speed downwind as he went on to win the regatta, but rather than go up and scrap for the windward position and join the queue of slower boats, he elected to sail a lower but parallel course some 6–10 lengths to leeward. Once in clear air, Glas was able to pull through some 5–6 boats each reach. But what was key was that he maintained his low, parallel course right to the mark and then gybed early, turning a 90° corner, and came up to the mark for a close rounding. The first time I witnessed the technique I thought he was going to sail straight past the mark, so different was the German's approach to the buoy.

However, it was a very effective method of avoiding all the disturbed air as fleets concertina at the mark (see Fig 7.1).

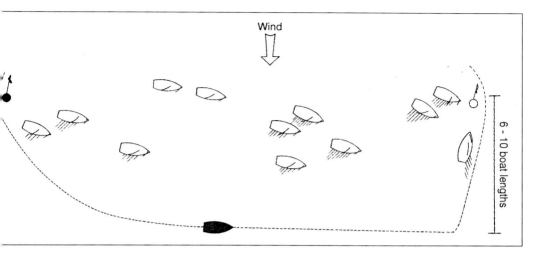

Fig 7.1 *Sail low on the reach to avoid all the dirty air from the boats to windward when caught on the outside of the mark or when trying to pass slower boats ahead. Do not sail back into the dirty air at the gybe mark, but maintain a parallel course and turn the corner well to leeward of the mark; then come up hard and fast to round the mark in clearer air.*

Overlaps at the mark

Approaching the downwind turning marks in company, the battle is on for the inside berth. The overlap rule is one of the most misquoted in the whole of the rule book. Any overlap has to be established 'When she (the outside overlapped yacht) comes within two of her overall lengths of a mark' (IYRR 42.1). Do not try to establish an overlap too soon, say at 15–20 lengths out from the mark because the outside boat will then have plenty of time to try to break it before the two lengths. The hardest occasion to judge an overlap is when surfing conditions exist and the boat that suddenly catches a wave right can pull out two lengths in as many seconds. Ensure the whole crew know when it is vital to make or hold an overlap, so that everyone on board can concentrate on making sure it happens. Pump the sails (once per wave and only when surfing or planning is possible (IYRR 54.3.) to make the overlap just before the outside boat enters the two lengths circle. When trying to avoid an inside yacht from gaining an overlap, bear off hard before the circle to angle the transom up to windward to reduce the overlap. At the same time the tactician, standing at the back of the boat, should make a big spectacle of sighting the over-lap and calling 'No overlap' (Fig 7.2). Many races incorrectly call 'No water' in this instance, which is in fact wrong; they could end up being protested for denying water. The reason is that if the inside boat disputes the existence of an overlap, you as the outside yacht have no choice but to grant them water and then protest, the onus then being on the inside boat to prove an overlap existed. In other words, you cannot refuse the inside boat water, and by shouting 'No water' you are in fact denying them their rights under IYRR 42.1, whereas what you really mean is, 'No overlap'.

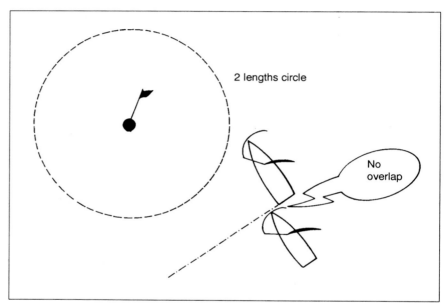

2 lengths circle

No overlap

Fig 7.2 *If fighting to prevent an inside overlap, try bearing off just before the two length circle to angle your transom ahead of the inside boat's bow.*

Once it has been agreed that an overlap exists, the pressure is off the inside boat a little and she can take her time and set up to make a good mark rounding, using the full two lengths circle to do so if she wishes. If the boat in front bears off to make a wide slow rounding, there can some-times be a small, tempting gap for a boat close astern to nip through if they are quick. It pays here to know how smart the other boat is, since experienced tactical sailors and those with match racing experience may well try such a manoeuvre as a baited trap. They wait until you are com-mitted with your bow between them and the mark, and then suddenly luff up hard and force you on to the mark. The last time I tried it at a world championship I was caught out, so be warned! Finally, beware of people that come into the bottom mark on starboard gybe shouting 'Starboard' at

Fig 7.3 *A ends the run ahead of B by gybing on each wind shift and actually sails less distance despite gybing more.*

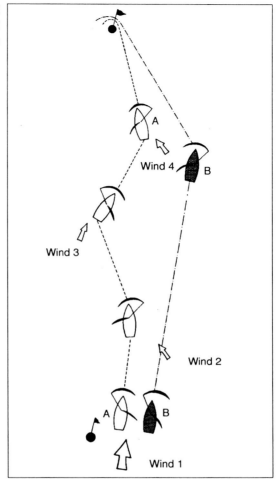

you. There is no such thing as starboard right of way once you are at two lengths from the mark, only the right of water for the inside, overlapped yacht.

Picking the gybes on the run

Every sailor should know the saying 'Windshifts do not stop at the windward mark', yet few racers gybe as often as they tack upwind. This is surprising in light of the fact that a yacht loses less speed gybing than it does tacking. Choosing the right shifts on the run simply means that you end up sailing less distance to the bottom mark (see Fig 7.3).

If the tactician is unsure of which gybe to come away on from the windward mark, there is a useful rule of thumb. If the boat was lifted into the mark, you need to gybe on to starboard to take advantage of the shift and run lower and closer to the next mark (assuming a port rounding). Tactically you may wish to work towards a particular side of the course to pick up or cheat the tidal stream or because there is more breeze on that side. Depending on the degree of benefit to be had, wait for a favourable shift to take you that way if possible, rather than sailing further distance to get there. Otherwise you may lose just as much as you gain.

Detecting windshifts downwind is a lot harder than upwind, with no headsail or tell-tales to telegraph the fact. The best source of information is the spinnaker trimmer, who just like the genoa trimmer upwind should feel and react to every gust or shift that hits the sail. When a lift arrives the trimmer should be the first to spot it. He checks that it is not just the helmsman steering low for a moment, and then informs the tactician in case he is looking for an opportunity to gybe. Time your gybes to spend as little time on the layline as possible, just as you would on the beat, to keep the options open and be able to make use of any useful windshifts that might come down. Avoid running too low into the bottom mark, as it places you at risk from boats reaching in from astern and leeward with more speed, who could easily establish a last minute overlap.

Before he calls each gybe the tactician needs to think through the 'What if' scenario of what the other boats around you are likely to do in response to your gybe. Is the boat behind just about to gybe and come across your stern, in which case it would pay to go before them to prevent them taking your wind and more importantly – to stop them getting inside you and then claiming the inside berth at the mark? Tactically the game is to pick the gybes to give you the fastest angles for the boat down to the mark, arriving as the inside boat and all the time sailing in clear air. Simple really!

Selecting the favoured end of the finish line

Never underestimate the importance of finding the favoured end of the finish line; just as you would not ignore bias on the starting line. Get it right, and if boats around you get it wrong, you could enjoy a last minute windfall of a better than expected position. Handicap racers plugging up the last beat on their own should not forget the benefits on offer either, despite the lack of opposition breathing down their necks. Once ashore with the results in their hands, a few seconds less could have meant you finishing a place higher.

Conservative covering tactics generally result in a course towards the middle of the beat for the final upwind leg, unless there is only one boat to cover who decides to take you out to the corner. Try to shepherd the boats astern together and towards the middle of the course to minimise the risk of yachts taking fliers off to the wings and finding a useful shift, by tacking below rather than on top of the boats you wish to follow you.

When defending your position strongly avoid the laylines. If a yacht tacks on top of you, you will have no option but to sit there and suffer it all the way to the line. Keep well between the laylines and you keep the options open. If a starboard tacker comes across, aim to duck astern, because if you tack to leeward he will invariably carry you on to the layline and beyond. If the boot is on the other foot and you are the one being tightly covered, try to push the opposition out to the layline and towards the unfavoured end of the line, in the hope that they will not like it and tack off, breaking the cover.

It is best to get fairly close to the line before it is possible to accurately read any bias, as the eyes do not have a built in range finder. I used to get it wrong often, largely from trying to read a small bias from too far down the track. What you need to ascertain is if one end of the line is further downwind than the other and therefore less distance to sail. It helps to judge it from directly downwind of the line as it is then a relatively simple matter of estimating if the buoy or committee boat end is nearer to you. Calling it from one side of the beat can be a lot tougher, as one end will always look further away and you can fool yourself into thinking it is more upwind when in reality you just can't see it so clearly. In this situation it is best to wait until you can spot the flags on the committee boat, the trailing edge of which will point to the favoured end (Fig 7.4).

The finish of the last race of the Dragon Gold Cup in Ostend in 1992 will be painfully ingrained in my memory for years. Crewing for the Danish double Olympic gold medallist, Poul Richard Hoj Jensen, we had success-

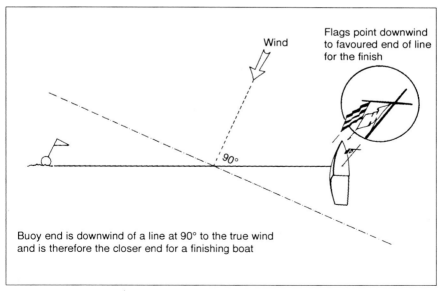

Fig 7.4 *The direction of the flags points to the favoured end of the line.*

fully covered our only possible rival for the championship, the German Star sailor Vincent Hoesh. He was a couple of places astern but safely behind on points. Approaching the finish in about fourth or fifth place we were gaining rapidly on the boats head. I could see that Poul Richard had decided it was safe to leave Vincent and I sensed he wanted to have a go at winning the final race, although the cup was already his. As we neared the line, Poul Richard asked me which end of the line was favoured. After peering at the line for several seconds, I nervously pronounced my findings, realising full well the implications of getting it wrong. 'Yes, it's definitely the buoy end,' I said, praying I was right. At this stage we could have perhaps won the race but certainly claimed second behind a Dutch boat.

As we tacked to lay the port end of the line a rival Danish sailmaker ducked astern of us and held on to the right and then the third placed German boat crossed behind also. We were now second, and if I had got the bias right we had a chance of snatching a first – it was that close. But as we got nearer to the mark, we seemed to be headed off to leeward. Suddenly I realised we were not going to lay it. We tacked in a hurry a couple of lengths short of the line and slowly inched towards the buoy. The breeze had dropped and the tidal stream had swung around and built dramatically since the last beat; we were now struggling to lay the down tide end of the line. The disaster rapidly turned into a nightmare as we were forced to tack again to avoid hitting the mark. The gun fired three times in rapid succession as further up the line the boats that stood on reached in over the line with speed. Boats seemed to be all over us and we finally cleared the line and headed for the harbour in silence; there were eight boats in front of ours. The most crucial call of the race and I had got it wrong.

When the results came out we had actually finished fourth, the bow having crossed the line and then slipped back on the tide some time before we finally cleared the line, and we had taken the regatta by some 22 points.

Rerunning the closing stages of the race in my mind, I was convinced that the port end of the line was further downwind, but what I had failed to take into account was that the tide had moved round and gained strength so much. In that part of the North Sea the tide swings through 180° or so, rather then flowing in one direction, declining then building from the opposite direction. I had checked the tide before the start as usual, but it is hard to keep track of it on the open sea with no instruments until we came across a moored buoy, and by then it was all too late. Although we had won the Gold Cup, I knew Poul would have loved to seal it by winning the last race. So the moral of the tale is: never forget the tide!

In a close finish, one-design sailors will always shoot the line, luffing the boat perpendicular to the line in order to put the bow over a second or so earlier than would have been the case had they kept on sailing straight.

Finishing towards one end of the line makes it easier to judge the exact second to luff the boat. One good helmsman I sailed with on an IOR One Tonner was very keen on this trick, and had picked it up in his successful dinghy racing days. As the boat came to the line he would call for the entire crew on the rail to rock their upper bodies aft, just like you would in a Laser dinghy to encourage the bow to luff up over a wave without having to use so much rudder. Whether it works on a 40 foot yacht is another matter, but the psychological effect of the whole crew trying so hard to push the boat over the line a second faster was great for moral!

Part 3: THE CAMPAIGN

8. Organising the Campaign

Planning the programme

When it comes to planning the season's campaign the first thing you need is a year planner chart. Together with the main crew members, mark in whichever event is the primary objective and work backwards from there. How much preparation you can fit in before your chosen event will clearly depend on the time available to the crew and the budget of the owner. If the ultimate aim is a world championship, the Rolex Commodore's Cup or a similar level international event I would wish to do at least two full international regattas a few weeks beforehand. Our campaign aboard a 38 foot racer cruiser (IMX 38) for Ford Cork Week one year began with a south coast spring series of seven races and a few days tune-up during March and April and then a weekend's training and race in the middle of June prior to the Cork Week regatta in July.

Good crew are always in demand, and as we saw in the first chapter sailors will often race on several different boats throughout the season. For this reason it is important to book your team early, get them to commit to the selected programme of weekend regattas and then confirm it in writing by sending them all a printed sailing programme with all the dates and times of races and practice days well in advance. A year ahead is not too early for major events, but at the latest your plans should be in place by January. Yacht racers lead busy lives and have to plan early for their time off work and which regattas they can fit in. Do not expect to be able to find a good crew a few weeks before the regatta; all the crew worth having will have been signed up months ago. During my sailmaking days it was amazing how many people would ring me at the end of the week looking for crew for that weekend which they expected me to be able to provide. My big red phone book has long since fallen apart!

The more important the event, the more care you will need to take in planning the build-up. Do not be tempted to cram too much sailing in just before the big event or you could arrive there jaded and burnt out. On the other hand, don't make the mistake I was forced into a few years back when time off was tight, of turning up with crew at a world championship having only raced together in three national events much earlier in he year. Top international events can be a significant step up from regional championships – ask the British teams at the 1994 Commodore's Cup! Even the experts need some exposure to the likely level of competition to remind them of what it is like, to test boatspeed and to relearn the different set of priorities demanded at such a level.

As an example, at regional events you may be used to getting the best starts and feel happy that you can get the boat off the line with the best of them. However, when you roll up at the world championship with, say 60 boats as well or better sailed than yours, the starts are not so easy. No more reaching into the line at speed, head up and off; these guys are lining up right on the line at two minutes to go, sails flapping, fighting for their positions. With 60 boats stacked up it is very hard to get to exactly where you wish to start. Having fought for a position on the front row, you then have to accelerate the boat from standing without being caught over the line early and without being rolled by the boats on either side; altogether a different ball game.

It may also be an idea to try out the regatta venue in advance if it is famous for localised current or wind conditions. Dennis Connor sailed the 1993 Etchells 22 European Championships and the 1994 UK Open event, both in the Solent on the English south coast, in preparation for the 1996 World Championship to be held there. So concerned was he about the local conditions that he hired two-time Olympic Gold medallist and local expert Rodney Pattisson as his coach.

Whatever level you are racing at and however expert your crew, we all need to spend time in the boat familiarising ourselves with new gear or changes in the crew before we go racing. A Saturday afternoon before a local Sunday race is perfect, but five minutes before the start of the first race is not the time to find out that the No 3 genoa will not fit the headfoil, or that the bowman has not done a dip-pole gybe before.

Crew selection

The only down side to big boat racing can be the hassle and time required to co-ordinate and keep happy some 10–14 different crew. They all need to feel involved and a vital part of the team, although a couple may know they are really only there for their weight. Right from the beginning the skipper and crew boss need to put together a team they think will get on, both on and off the boat. This is the most important criterion for selection, even ahead of ability and experience, for if the crew does not gel into a team they will get nowhere.

One piece of perhaps surprising advice is not to pick someone who is too good for the boat. Persuading the trimmer off last year's championship winner to come and sail aboard your new boat in her first series with an inexperienced crew may not always work. The hot shot can easily become frustrated if he/she is not at his/her accustomed place at the front of the fleet and the rest of the crew may not appreciate being shouted at or being told what to do by a newcomer on the boat. Not all 'Pros' are like that of course, but enthusiastic youngsters who have sailed on well organised boats often then think that all yacht racing is like that and expect the next campaign they move onto to be the same.

When assembling the crew select a level of ability to match the job specification of the position concerned. The most experienced sailors should fill the bow, trimmer, mainsheet, helmsman and tactician roles. These are the key positions which have the greatest control over boat handling and speed. The next best guys are needed at the mast, in the 'pit', on the grinders, runners and navigating – if this is a separate role from the tactician's. The 'B max' or pure ballast crew can be relatively inexperienced or else dinghy sailors keen to have a ride on a big boat. They should know their way around a boat and be capable of pulling strings if required, but for most of the time there will be little for them to do other than hike out. For someone who believes themselves to be worthy of more than such a limited 'job spec' it can be very annoying and frustrating not to be contributing more to the race and they will soon become bored. Choose people who will be grateful for the opportunity just to sit on the side and be part of the team. It can be the ideal position for the owner's guest and visitors or novice crew you are keen to bring on.

The right person for the job

The size and layout of the yacht will dictate the number of crew and the division of labour between them. The bigger the boat and the greater the

Boat size	Total crew	Positions
28 ft	5	Bow, mast/pit, 2 trimmers, helm/mainsheet/tactician
30 ft	6	Bow, mast/pit, 2 trimmers, mainsheet, helm/tactician
33 ft	7	Bow, mast/pit, 2 trimmers, mainsheet, helm, tactician
35 ft	8	Bow, mast/pit, 2 trimmers, mainsheet, helm, tactician
38 ft	9–10	Bow, mast/pit, grinder, 2 trimmers, mainsheet, helm, tactician, runners
40 ft	10–11	Bow, mast/pit, grinder, 2 trimmers, mainsheet, helm, tactician, navigator, runners
(Plus 1–3 for extra ballast in heavy airs).		

crew, the more specific a job specification each will have. The table on page 110 describes the common allocation of duties across a typical range of boat sizes.

How you organise the exact division of responsibilities on the boat will depend upon the skill and experience of the crew available. The table shows how on smaller yachts some doubling up of roles is inevitable, but let's look at the job description for each position on the boat in turn so that you can find the right individual for each job. We'll also see how the division of responsibilities is split up amongst a race crew.

Bow

Ideal weight: under 70 kg (the lighter the better)
Ideal height: 1.73–1.78 m
Physical attributes: low centre of gravity useful!

The bow person (this can be a good position for women on smaller boats) needs to be fit and highly mobile. Good upper body strength is also required when the role doubles up with the mast position, as this involves bouncing halyards. The archetypal bowman is small, wiry and able to climb the mast at a moment's notice. However, on boats that use the end-for-end gybe technique the bowman has to be tall enough to reach the pole end on the mast. For race boats that use the dip-pole gybe system the mastman can be used to raise the inboard end of the pole up the mast prior to the gybe, although many boats now have the spinnaker pole car adjusted on a continuous control line, so lack of height is not a problem.

Areas of responsibility

The bowman should always check (and re-pack if necessary) all the headsails and spinnakers before every race. In the heat of the race, it is the bowman who will receive the abuse if a spinnaker goes up twisted, so it is in his best interest to check the pack. Many a bowman will refuse to let any other crew member rig up the sheets and guys in his 'office'. The fore-deck hand should always do this for himself and then check again just before the start for any sheet lead the wrong side of a stanchion or guard rail, or perhaps the twinning line being left off.

At the start, it is the bowman's job to signal to the helmsman the distance to go to the line. He needs to get himself a good transit on the line beforehand so that he can be confident in his call. Confirm with the helm the system of hand signals to be used. Usually the number of fingers raised indicates boatlengths to go to the line, a fist held horizontally means on the line, and the thumbs down signal indicates that the boat is over.

As far as maintenance is concerned, the bowman should keep the pole end fittings rinsed free of salt after each outing and well lubricated. If the guy pops out of the pole end after the gybe it will be the bowman's job to fix it. He should also keep an eye on the headfoil, to ensure no sharp edges develop to rip the luff tape, or wear in the luff groove which can allow the tape to pull out when the sail is pulled down.

The bowman's role

Once the headsail has been dropped on an offwind leg the bowman, with back-up from the mastman, should always bag the sail and pull it off the fore deck, back to the mast. Even if the sail is likely to be used again on the next leg a good fore deck crew will always bag the sail in case a change of wind speed at the leeward mark demands a last minute change of head-sail. Another reason not to leave the No 3 headsail on the foredeck during an Olympic triangle race is that if the wind shifts and the second reach becomes too shy for the kite, the No 1 or No 2 headsail will be needed in a hurry. Leaving the previous sail on deck, catching every wave, can add up to a lot of water and hence weight being held just where you do not want it. Having slippery wet sails flaked on the deck can also make gybing the pole a hazardous operation for the fore deck crew.

When dropping the headsail always try to pull the sail down by grip-ping the luff tape below the bottom pre-feeder so as not to rip the luff tape out of the luff groove, which invariably cuts a slice out of the plastic foil.

The bowman calls the distance to the start line by using hand signals.

Immediately after the drop, the bowman should be in the habit of clipping the genoa halyard on to the tack fitting so that the mast can be pulled forward. This is critical on yachts with an in-line rig, as the mast head can be pulled up and forward a considerable distance, improving downwind speed no end. Boats with swept back rigs are not able to pull their mast forward anything like as much, due to the aft pull of the shrouds and lowers, but it is still worth trying. As the pitman winds the rig forward on the winch, the bowman, on his way back to the rail, should eyeball the mast as it goes forward to check that the spar is absolutely straight and not inverted. Always have someone monitor the mast in this way when it is being wound forward, or something expensive might happen! Check there is still some tension in the runner to prevent the mast from bouncing around.

When the call comes from the back of the boat selecting the headsail for the next leg, the pitman passes the bagged sail up on to the deck, into the hands of the bowman on the rail, who then splits the bag open at both ends to attach the halyard and sheets. The sail, still in its bag, can be held on the rail until the call comes to plug it in to the headstay. The choice of which luff groove to use may be called from the afterguard if they think there is a likelihood of a change on the next beat. It is best to organise things for an inside hoist when changing genoas so that the boat never stops driving off the new sail once up

The bowman needs to keep track of all the halyards in use at the top of the mast and try to keep them uncrossed. Obviously halyards can jam when crossed and can only be cleared by a trip up the mast. Occasionally this will mean telling the tactician or crew boss 'No,' when there is a call for a hoist which would involve getting halyards wrapped tightly around the headfoil or when not enough halyards are available to use. A spinnaker peel, for instance, requires 3 halyards to effect.

Peeling the spinnaker

The bowman should ensure the boat carries a peeling strop, fitted with spinnaker clips at both ends. When the call comes to peel to a new kite, the sail is passed up to the bowman who clips on the spare halyard. He then attaches the strop on to the clew which goes forward, and the other end on to either a change sheet or the lazy guy detached from the currently flying sail. The other end of the peeling strop can be either clipped on to the tack fitting or to a solid part of the fore-stay if the sail is to be set fairly broad in heavy airs. In lighter conditions the bowman should go to the end of the spinnaker pole and attach the strop there. This involves the intrepid fore deck hand climbing the pole while attached to the third halyard by his climbing harness. If the boat is close reaching, the strop should always be connected to the spinnaker pole end; as the pole will be within reach of the bow. Alternatively, two snap shackles joined together

The mastman needs both height and strength to raise the halyards up the mast easily.

may be used instead. The new sail is then best hoisted inside the old and set flying off the strop and change sheet. The bowman then fires off the old guy by having the pole dropped in to him at the bow. He then re-connects the sheet and guy to the new sail and finally fires off the peeling strop. If, instead, the strop is led to the pole end and the bowman is of the more athletic variety, the old kite should be fired off from the pole end whilst the bowman is still at the end of the pole.

Every time a spinnaker is dropped during a race, it is the bowman's responsibility to clear the pole off the mast and clip the topping lift down to the base of the mast so that the boat is free to tack. Often, as the boat comes around the bottom mark in a tightly bunched fleet, there is a split second opportunity to tack just after the mark into clean air. The bowman needs to be quick to clear the fore-deck otherwise the window of opportunity will be closed by the boat astern rounding the mark and getting his bow up inside yours and so preventing you from tacking straight away.

A quick and capable bowman is worth his weight in gold; or in beer at least! As we have seen there are a multitude of manoeuvres he needs to be familiar with so that whatever the call and however late the call may come, the job can be done as quickly and smoothly as possible. A good bowman can make the rest of the crew look good – or just very ordinary – during gybes and drops. Finding an experienced crew to run the bow should be one of the first priorities of crew selection.'

Mastman

Ideal weight: 76–82 kg
Ideal height: 1.67 m plug

The mastman is usually a taller and heavier specimen than the bowman, as he needs a good reach to 'top' the pole and grab halyards from whatever height they may exit the mast. A good technique combined with good upper body strength is necessary for the rapid 'bouncing' or hoisting of halyards. The hand-over-hand method of hoisting is twice as quick as using two hands together, but does demand more strength when the load comes on when the sail is nearly up. The best technique is to place your foot against the mast with a bent leg and then straighten the leg in time with the pull down, so pushing away from the rig and bringing more of the halyard with you. Call to the trimmers when the sail, genoa or spinnaker is 2 metres from fully hoisted, so that they can begin to bring the sheet in as soon as the sail is up and drawing.

Other than operating the halyards and spinnaker pole height on the mast, the mastman's role is to back up the bowman on the fore deck with packing headsails, clipping on the sheets, and helping change the pole and sheets and guys over. Backing up the bow also means lending a hand

The mastman needs to watch and communicate closely with the bowman in order to work in sympathy with him.

when the bowman looks likely to run out of time before a manoeuvre. He should not normally need to venture on the foredeck, especially if the bowman is already up there, but can carry out his role perfectly well from up by the mast where his weight will not hurt fore-and-aft trim.

Ideally, whoever gets the job of managing the mast will have past experience of running the bow, so he knows exactly what is involved in each manoeuvre. This is desirable for two reasons:

1 So that he can support the bowman smoothly and efficiently without being asked, say, to take up the slack on the halyard as the headsail is plugged in, or to reroute the sheets through the No 3 cars when changing down to the No 3 jib.
2 So that he can take over the bowman's job at a moment's notice should the bowman be injured or, more likely, be required for any specialist lightweight job such as climbing the mast to recover lost halyards or repairing a ripped spinnaker below.

Whilst hiking out upwind, the mastmen will sit at number 2 position on the rail and is ideally sited to call the waves and wind speed fluctuations for the helmsman and trimmers. Similarly, he can pass information forward to the bow, who in heavy air can often hear nothing from the back of the boat, due to having his head buried in a wave for much of the time.

Pit

Ideal weight: 76–86 kg
Ideal height: Any

If you thought the pit position was a fairly low key job and somewhere to place an inexperienced crew member, you are mistaken. The pitman is often the key to successful boat handling, because if a sail does not go up or down fast enough or at the right time it is the pitman who has his hand on the end of the halyard. The pit can also make or break a smooth gybe as it is he who controls the height of the pole as it is dropped in to the bowman on a dip-pole gybe. Similarly he will operate the up and downhaul during an end-for-end gybe.

The pitman's role can be described as the management of all halyards plus mainsail control lines such as the outhaul, kicker (vang), cunningham and possibly the leech line if led forward. The precise location of each of these controls will vary from boat to boat, and so it is a matter of ergonomics to work out which member of the crew sits within reach of each control and is free to operate it at the time required. In the case of the Dubois 40 foot *Impulse* pictured on the front cover, the cunningham, in-haul (the mainsail clew was fixed) and checkstays were all led back under the deck to the mainsail trimmer's position and can just be seen in the photo under the mainsheet trimmer's left knee.

Beginning with the basics of the job, the pitman obviously needs to know where all the halyards are led. Clutches should be clearly labelled, not for his use as he will know them inside out, but for the benefit of the rest of the crew. Invariably if some other crew member is asked to release an unmarked clutch in the heat of a mark rounding, the main halyard comes down.

Efficient operation of halyard clutches entails some method of minimising rope slippage. If a halyard slips during the race, the pitman should have a contingency arrangement in place, such as leaving the halyard tail around the cabin top winch. It is generally the higher loaded No 3 and No 4 headsails which cause most creep and sometimes the main halyard in heavy air. There have been numerous advances in rope clutch design to overcome these problems, but you need to ensure the clutch is suitable for the type and diameter of line in use and be sure to replace the halyard with one of similar diameter when it is time for renewal.

Other tricks of the trade to extend the life of a halyard are to end-for-end it halfway through the season to change the point of wear inside the clutch, or have covers sewn over the rope at the point at which the clutch grips the halyard. It is the pitman's responsibility to ensure that the rope clutches do their job effectively, and if they do not, to get them changed.

The pitman's job does not stop when he is out of the pit and sitting on the rail. Every time the yacht tacks, he should take with him across the boat the tails of the control lines he may need to adjust upwind, eg main outhaul, cunningham and genoa halyard. Operating these control lines from out on the rail is much better than disrupting the boat by having to leave the rail and climb into the middle of the boat. Even controls on the opposite side of the boat may be adjusted if led around the leeward halyard winch up on to the rail. If small adjustments to trim require a man off the rail to carry them out, then any benefit to boatspeed may easily be lost by the detrimental effect of the temporary loss of weight on the rail. This is especially true when operating the kicker on a windy close reach, and is one reason why the control lines for the vang should be lead well outboard down both sides of the boat, to within reach of the pitman's position on the rail.

The fundamental law of working the pit is to look at the end of whatever string you are pulling. Simple as it may sound, there are far too many pitmen that do not. Watch the bowman as you tail the halyard when the headsail is plugged into the foil, so that you do not pull the sail out of his hands. Carry a marker pen so that the halyards, outhaul and cunningham can all be marked for the day's conditions and the settings reproduced exactly for the subsequent windward legs. When it comes to dropping the spinnaker, the halyard should be neatly flaked and ready to run free. Rope tails, bags or nets just inside the companionway can be a big help in keeping the tails tangle free.

The best sail trimmers are those that keep their eyes glued to the sail and can concentrate all day. Photo: *Frazer Clark.*

Below decks, the pitman is responsible for the stowage of sails so that:

- The weight distribution is in the right place, over the keel.
- The sails are arranged in order, so that the ones likely to be used first are readily available. Tie a sail tie on to the spinnaker bag and leave it hanging out on deck so that the kite can be grabbed from on deck.

Sail trimmer

Ideal weight: 80 kg plus
Ideal height: 1.78 m plus

The sail trimmer's role is one that requires a good deal of experience and technical knowledge of how to get the best speed out of the sails in every condition. Sure, it is relatively easy to set the leads up correctly and trim the headsail so that the tell-tales all lift together, but there are a wealth of more advanced techniques involved, such as how to cope with wind shear, trimming for waves and pulses in wind strength, co-ordinating with the helmsman, all of which make the difference between an average trimmer and a good one.

The best sail trimmers have an attention span that lasts all day (and all night when required in offshore races) and during that time can keep changing gear for every single oscillation in wind speed or direction. They should have an open mind, be keen to learn and experiment, and always be searching for ways to make the boat go faster. An 'average' trimmer is quite happy to stand on the side of the boat downwind with the spinnaker sheet motionless in his hand. As long as the kite flies steadily without collapsing he is happy that he is doing his job adequately. To my mind, if the sheet is not moving constantly, if the winch is not constantly clicking, then the trimmer is not working hard enough. The kite should always be on the edge of collapse. At broad angles the trimmer should generally be seeking to sneak the pole back whenever the wind angle allows him to create a greater projected area.

Physically, the ideal cockpit crew is a big, broad shouldered guy who can get his body over the winch and bring the sail in swiftly through the tack. He needs to have good cardio-vascular fitness to cope with extended tacking duels and heavy air spinnaker legs. Technically he needs to know not only how to set up the headsail for optimum VMG but also to have a feel for how his sail is affecting the mainsail and pressure on the helm. It is no good the genoa trimmer strapping in the heavy No 1 at the top end of its range and thinking 'Well, my sail looks OK,' only to watch the mainsail lifting so much that it blows inside out as a result of the excessive lee side pressure. The experienced and confident trimmer will communicate frequently with the helmsman about boatspeed and wind angle and secondly with the mainsheet trimmer to ensure the genoa is in balance with the main.

Knowing the relative ability and experience of the two trimmers will help the skipper decide on which system to operate in the cockpit. If the trimmers are equally skilled then it is best if they take a side of the boat each so that one of the pair does not get worn out by grinding all day. Motivation and attention spans can be maintained longer if the trimmers are rested in turn, and a friendly spirit of competition as to which tack can achieve the higher numbers is no bad thing. On the other hand, if one is obviously more expert than the other and it is only a short inshore race, you may decide to have the best crew trimming the whole time whilst the other tails through the tacks and takes the guy downwind.

Whichever way the cockpit is organised, the priorities are to have the minimum number of crew off the rail before and after the tack and for them not to be fighting each other for space in the cockpit. Work out the ergonomics of the tack so that the trimmers do not have to pass each other during its execution. The order of tacking should be something like this:

Trimmer 1 – Moves down the windward rail, ready to let off the headsail.
Trimmer 2 – Remains on rail.
Helmsman – Gives order to tack.
Trimmer 1 – Eases one foot of sheet as the helm goes over and spins the rest off the winch after the bow is well past head-to-wind.
Trimmer 2 – Now on the leeward side, tails in the new genoa sheet.
Trimmer 1 – Turns around from the old winch and takes the tail of its sheet from behind Trimmer 2, then climbs backwards onto the rail, still tailing.

Trimmer 2 – Grasps the winch handle and winds in rapidly. When the
sheet is nearly in, takes the sheet from Trimmer 1 (who by now has his
legs out on the rail) by calling 'Mine.'

Trimmer 2 – Squeezes in the last few inches of sheet only when the boat
is up to speed. Checks final trim and moves swiftly to the windward rail
if weight is required. On his way across the cockpit, he prepares the
windward genoa winch by pulling through the slack in the sheet and
loads the winch drum with just three turns and puts the handle in.

When it comes to gybing in all but the heaviest of air, the sheet trimmer should move into the middle of the boat and take the sheet and guy
in either hand. It is much easier for one person to co-ordinate the critical
timing of the spinnaker passing across the front of the boat in an effort to
keep it flying through the manoeuvre. In heavy airs or on a reach to reach
gybe a separate trimmer will be required on both the sheet and guy in
order to handle the load.

Ideally, the tactician should tell the trimmers well before the boat
reaches the top mark what the likely wind angle for the next leg will be.
If it is to be a white-sailer, the trimmer is then responsible for rigging an
outboard sheet before the boat has borne off on to the reach.

The trimmers, often being larger members of the crew, need to be aware
at all times of the position of their weight around the cockpit. In hiking
conditions, when a change of sail trim is required, it will be quicker for the

*When the genoa trimmer is hiking on the rail, it is often easier and quicker for
the mainsheet trimmer to nip down to leeward to make small adjustments to the
genoa trim.* Photo: *Ocean Images.*

genoa trimmer to remain on the rail and the mainsheet hand to nip across the cockpit to adjust the sheet (Photo on page 120). When it is necessary for the trimmer to sit at the winch and trim continually, he should try to get his weight to windward by cross sheeting, which should also give him a better view of the front of the headsail.

Mainsail trimmer

Ideal weight: 82 kg plus

Physically the mainsail trimmer needs to be fit and strong in the upper body, especially in the shoulders and arms, in order to cope with long hours of playing the traveller upwind. The back and leg muscles can also get weary from prolonged sitting at strange angles with the muscles held in constant tension. The trimmer's cardio-vascular rate (heart and lung capacity) needs to be high, especially when racing aboard older boats with high friction block and tackle mainsheet systems that can be hard work.

Technically, the mainsail trimmer should know what shape is needed to make the boat go fast for each wind speed. This demands a good grounding in the principles of sail trim, together with a good eye for sail shape, so that the trimmer can not only recognise a sail that is too flat, too full, too closed, too open etc, but knows what remedial measures would rectify the problem.

Upwind, apart from being in charge of a major element of the yacht's speed, the main trimmer also has control of the degree of helm carried by the rudder. He can, in effect, help steer the boat by the position of the traveller and the tension of the leech. He needs to be aware of this and should keep glancing back from time to time to see at what angle the tiller or wheel is to the centreline of the boat. If the helmsman is struggling to bear off with the tiller up around his ear, this is an indication that the mainsail needs to be twisted off or dropped down the traveller some more. Four degrees of windward helm and no more is what you are looking for upwind, and none downwind. Two lines drawn on the cockpit floor beneath the tiller at four degrees to the centreline is a useful reference, or coloured tape on the top of the wheel can be used in a similar way.

In addition to having his hands full with the mainsheet and traveller control line, the mainsail trimmer is also in charge of the cunningham, outhaul, kicker (vang), main halyard tension, leechline, runner tension, checkstay and backstay, and should know which of the crew to call upon to operate them for him.

One main responsibility for the mainsail trimmer is to dump the mainsheet quickly at mark roundings and in sympathy with the helmsman, who cannot turn the boat until the mainsail is eased out. The trimmer has to be ready for this with the mainsheet out of the cleat in time (or out of the self-tailer if it is a winched system) and aggressively force the sail out. Often the main trimmer cannot see the approaching mark from the windward

When rounding a mark or when a gust strikes, the mainsheet trimmer needs to be able to dump all the mainsail in a hurry.

side, so it is important for the tactician to call the boatlengths into the mark. Similarly, if there is a call to dip a starboard tack yacht upwind, the helmsman cannot bear off until the main is eased. If the main does not go out, the trimmer will not be very popular!

Before the race, the mainsheet hand should ensure the battens are all tightly secured in their pockets, and may well have a choice to make over the flexibility of the top batten. In these days of full-length top battens, a stiff top batten will help hold the leech straight for a fair exhaust, but in light airs it will force too much depth into the head and create creases near the mast down-wind.

Runners

Operating the runners on a race boat with an in-line rig is a crucial role. Get it wrong and the rig comes down. The job requires someone who understands the importance of the task, is quick and nimble across the boat but with enough strength to wind up serious tension. The runner operator should ensure the genoa trimmer 'preps up' (the common term for loading the winch, pulling through the slack runner tail and fitting a handle in the winch) the new runner before leaving the leeward side. On the command 'Ready about', the runner man jumps down to leeward, shouts, 'Ready', and begins to take in the new runner as the bow passes through the wind. At that precise moment, the old runner is released, always gently and with a hand guiding the tail off the drum. The runner is then wound up to the prescribed tension for the prevailing wind speed. In light airs it is worth waiting for the boat to regain speed before the final tension is applied.

At the windward mark, it is the runner man's job to check that the leeward runner is removed from the winch and is free to run. The helmsman will not be able to bear off if the lee runner is pinning the main in. When gybing in light airs, someone needs to quickly run the old runner right forward so that the main boom is free to run out to the shrouds.

On masthead boats and cruiser racers with swept back rigs, the operation of the runner is not so crucial as the rigs have a greater safety margin built in. Here the runners or perhaps checkstays do not have to be brought in so quickly, and can be operated by another member of the crew; possibly the main trimmer or navigator. However, in a medium breeze and upward, when pointing ability is at a premium, it may be better to organise a dedicated runner operator to get the tension on quickly after the tack, so that the helmsman can steer up on to the wind as soon as possible.

Tactician

Ideal weight: Less than 75 kg

The tactician's role may be combined with that of the navigator's depending on the size of boat and talent available but for the purpose of detailing the job description we will look at each position separately.

The tactician's job is in fact very different from the rest of the crew who are involved in sail trimming and boat handling. The tactician does none of that, and instead of concentrating hard on the boat his concentration is focused away from it, on the opposition, the traffic ahead, looking for windshifts, monitoring the height and speed of nearby boats, and on a host of other information gathering clues.

His responsibilities begin before the boat even leaves the dock, when he needs to check that the race instructions, tidal information and weather forecast are all aboard. As soon as the yacht reaches the race area the tactician should be monitoring the wind direction and timing the period of any wind shifts. By noting down the direction and time every five minutes, he can ascertain whether the shifts are simply oscillating either side of a mean direction or if the breeze is persistently veering or backing.

This information is vital to the tactician's plans for the first beat. If the wind is oscillating, he can tell immediately after the start if the boat is on the high or low side of the mean and so whether or not to tack. If his monitoring of the wind before the start suggests a persistent shift, then that will dictate the boat's starting position in order to sail to the favoured side of the course to ensure being on the inside of the lift. Even if the wind is not shifting much, tracking the breeze is a good way of getting a feel for what the wind is likely to do during the course of the race.

Once the start line has been laid, the tactician should take the boat up on to the transit of the line, on the other side of the committee boat, and measure the angle of the line. Taking into account what he has just learned about the wind direction, and considering any forecast movement in the wind, the tactician decides on where to start and the planned route up the first beat.

As to who actually calls the start is really a matter for the helmsman and tactician to agree between themselves. Some helmsmen prefer to be told where to start and then be left alone to get on with it. Helms who have come up from dinghy and one-design classes are probably used to judging the start themselves. This is probably the best way, because often the helmsman will have to make a split second decision to go either above or below a boat, and there will not be time for a tactician to tell him which is the best option. However, if the tactician does call the start, he has the advantage of being able to look astern or nip down to leeward and see what gaps are in the line ahead: generally he has more time to look about and size up the situation.

If the helmsman is at all nervous at the start, or is inexperienced in big fleet starts, this is the favoured technique. I have used it at many regattas, and helmsmen who have previously proved to be nervous wrecks are completely happy to get right on to the line and mix it with the best, as long as someone else is calling the shots. As soon as you remove the responsibility for a good start from them, they cease to worry. Invariably, if you pull off an ace start, the tactician's input is somehow forgotten – but not if it was a bad one!

Out from the start, the tactician will be watching the wind shifts closely, and choosing the right shift to work out to the preferred side of the course. A good tactician, however, will not just tack the boat on the first good shift without first checking that the track is clear ahead, that the boat will not be in disturbed air on the new tack, and will not shortly have to tack again for any yacht on starboard. Whilst picking his way up the beat, the tactician also needs to keep an eye on the big picture of how the whole fleet is doing across the race course. Are the boats out to sea gaining? Is there a wind bend inshore off the cliffs? Is there more wind on the left? Is there a header up ahead? He will use all the possible indicators of change that there may be out on the course; the heading and angle of heel of any boats further upwind, the tide on passing buoys, the direction of smoke, or the formation of cloud over the land, to build up an understanding of what is actually happening at that time.

Downwind, the tactician's job is certainly not over. You have no doubt heard the saying 'Wind shifts do not stop downwind', and although they may he harder for the helmsman to pick up, the only real possibilities for gaining places downwind stem from exploiting the shifts correctly. It is a simple fact that if you gybe on each available shift, you end up sailing a shorter course to the mark. The 'tick-tack man' also needs to find time to look back up the track and see what the conditions are likely to be on the next leg, to consider his route up the beat, and to advise on the choice of sail.

Approaching the bottom mark, the tactician will have all sorts of decisions to make as to where to position the boat. Can we gain the overlap and round inside? Do we need room to tack immediately? Should we make an early or late kite drop? Mark roundings are often situations when the tactician's knowledge of the rules can be tested. For instance, if your boat is clear ahead, the tactician should call 'No overlap'. There is no such call as 'No water', and if there is a dispute, you have no choice but to give the other boat room and then protest. The tactician's golden rule is: Never take the boat into a situation where you cannot see a way out. This involves having a 'plan B' escape route out of a situation before committing the boat to a tricky manoeuvre, such as approaching the windward mark on the port layline.

Another important job the tactician is to know the race instructions inside out, so that if someone asks which is the finish line, or if there is a one minute rule, he can answer promptly, without having to dive below deck and spend ten minutes rummaging in the chart table. The good tacticians are easy to spot; they will be wearing a head-bearing compass around their necks to tell when the boat is on the layline into the mark. The layline will, in fact, vary depending on tidal strength, direction and boatspeed. In the Solent, 1.5–2.5 knots of tide can often mean adding an extra 5–15° on to the bearing of the layline.

After the race, the tactician should go over in his mind any tactical incidents that could have been handled better. New situations are often arising in yacht racing, such as a yacht with a symmetrical spinnaker running downwind being luffed by a boat sailing higher angles with an asymmetric kite. Suddenly there is no such thing as a 'proper course to the mark'. Some situations will crop up again and again on the water, depending on the type of racing you are involved in, so it is worth reading up on them and being prepared.

Lastly, if the boat is ever involved in a protest, it should be the tactician who fills in the form and attends the hearing. He should be the boat's rules expert, and the chances are he will have had most time to see the incident at first hand. It may be well worth carrying a cheap instamatic camera to snap overlaps or any ugly incidents that are likely to end up in the protest room.

Navigator

As much as 60 per cent of the navigator's job can be carried out ashore. The navigator needs to be a well prepared and disciplined type, with an eye for accuracy and to have the time available to fulfil all the pre-race preparation. His actual function will vary from race to race, depending upon the type and length of the course. On an Olympic course, his role will be to provide tidal information and bearing and distance to the next mark if it is not clearly visible. Longer inshore and offshore races require more traditional navigation in order to pinpoint marks accurately without over or understanding. But traditional methods of navigation are changing dramatically; with the growing use of electronic aids and instruments, such as GPS, chart plotters, tactical PC systems and weather fax receivers. The race boat navigator is nowadays to be found sitting on the rail at the back of the boat with a waterproof PC on his lap, rather than huddled over the chart table below with a paper chart and parallel rule trying to work out the course between the marks.

The navigator's responsibilities

Before the regatta or series commences, the navigator needs to check that the boat is equipped with not only properly calibrated instruments but also all the necessary tidal information; a tidal almanac, a tidal atlas and any local tide charts, such as the rotating plastic Solent guide, popularly known as the 'Wheel of Fortune'! If the race venue is new to the navigator, he should spend time ashore speaking to knowledgeable locals to pick up details of the tidal flow. In precisely which direction is the flow out of the harbour? Does it turn first inshore, and if so when? Are there any significant back eddies to consider? He should also ask about any local dangers, like hidden rocks, wrecks, outfalls, sandbanks or prohibited areas.

Racing in Ford Cork Week we enlisted the services of a good sailor from Crosshaven to be our 'local knowledge'. In the final harbour race, we ended up running in to the finish in very light airs along a rocky shore, to beat the foul tide. Our man directed us to creep right up into a small bay. Ahead was an outlying rock which rose a metre or so out of the water, which the helmsman aimed to skirt tightly round. However, 'local knowledge', as he became known, advised us that hidden just below the surface lurked a second rock, some six metres seaward. We watched in great anticipation as our rival ahead was gently luffed right on to the invisible rock, whilst we were able to avoid it safely. When their boat was lifted out there was a hole the size of a large fist in the front of the keel. That one incident was enough for us to finish above our rival overall, and shows the value of local information.

When racing around the cans, the navigator is responsible for noting down the course when it is announced at the 10 minute signal. He must quickly produce the list of marks with the magnetic bearing between each mark. If time is short, his first priority will be to tell the tactician and helmsman the magnetic bearing and distance to the first mark and secondly, advise the fore deck crew of the most likely gybe and angle of the first offwind leg, so that the pole and sheets can be set up on the correct

side before the start. Any sailor who has ever got a course wrong will recommend that two copies of the course are written down; the original to be
left on the chart table and a wet copy for the navigator to keep on deck.

Before announcing the course to the crew, check it makes sense logi-
cally by applying the 'piece of string test'. If a length of string was placed
around each of the marks on the chart and pulled taught, would it touch
each one? If it would not, the chances are that the course is wrong –
remember there is no such thing as a passing mark, unless it expressly says
so in the sailing instructions. The navigator then has to figure out if he
has taken the course down incorrectly or if the race committee has made
the mistake, which is not unheard of. 1994's infamous Cowes Week
Britannia Cup race made the headlines because the fleet were sent nearly
all the way to the Dean Tail buoy which, it transpired, had been lifted some
two years previously!

During the race, the navigator's job is to advise the helm and/or tactician on the quickest course to the mark, taking into account the tidal situation, and to call when the layline is approaching. It should be decided
amongst the afterguard whose job it is to call the layline, because if racing in close company there will be many tactical considerations to apply.

At mark roundings the navigator is the only person free to look at the
tide showing on the mark which he should use to compare with the tidal
atlas prediction. He should update the tactician every 15 minutes or so on
the tidal situation and just remind him if the boat's track inshore takes her

Here the navigator checks to see if the boat has reached the windward mark layline.

out of the favourable stream. The navigator also has a watching brief to be aware of any dangers up the track, such as shallow or prohibited areas.

Downwind the navigator's job is to keep the helmsman on track to the mark by frequently updating him on the cross track error, either from the GPS, Decca or compass.

It is best if the navigator can take responsibility for all the electronics on the boat, for the chances are that he will be the person that understands their operation the best. He obviously needs to ensure all the instruments are operating correctly and that they are calibrated regularly. This will involve reading up all the manuals and operating instructions. Charts, either paper or in the form of software cartridges, need to be kept up to date too.

Do not fall into the trap of fitting the latest electronic bit of kit the day before a major regatta and expecting to be totally *au fait* with the information at once. However wonderful the latest electronic gizmo may be, it will only improve the boat's performance if the information it produces is readily available and in a 'user friendly' form that the navigator can quickly assimilate. As an example, a straightforward GPS being used to locate racing marks in a short inshore race will only provide a lat and long fix. But for the helmsman, searching ahead for the gybe mark, to be told it is at 50 degrees 45.45 north and 01 degrees 11.13 west, in the heat of a short race, means very little. To be able to see the boat's track on the screen of a chart plotter, together with the complete course, submarine contours and tidal flows makes the same information much easier to understand in a hurry.

Helmsman

Ideal weight: 76–82 kg

Compared with all the other crew positions we have looked at, the helmsman's role is relatively simple. All he has to do is drive the boat fast and do what he is told! The main requirement is the ability to concentrate hard for long periods; he can simply not afford to look away from the tell-tales and water ahead for an instant. The best helms tend to say very little when driving the boat but are authoritative enough to clearly call tacks and gybes. If the helmsman has complete faith in his tactician he can relax into his own job without having to worry about where the boat is going, or if he is about to hit anything. Every time a helmsman looks to leeward at a converging boat, the boat starts to lose height. If a close starboard tacker is coming in, do not let the helm look at it until it is across tbe bows. Have the cockpit crew go down to leeward and call any dip necessary from there.

The helmsman needs an intuitive feel for the balance on the helm and also to feel when a change to trim will improve or reduce boat speed. They say the top guys should be able to feel the difference when the main clew outhaul is pulled out 30 mm! He needs to communicate with both main and headsail trimmers and feed back to them when the boat feels fast and if the weight distribution is right. He also needs to make it clear when he is sailing for speed and when sailing for height, so that the trimmers can shape the sails accordingly.

Skipper

The role of skipper of a modern race boat or racer cruiser has changed dramatically in recent times. Much like a captain of a football team, he can play in any position, and his actual influence upon a highly skilled team during the race should not need to be great. The skipper is becoming a nominal title and used to suggest someone that took all the decisions on board and barked orders to the crew. With an experienced and confident crew, the tactician takes care of all tactical calls and the crew boss co-ordinates the boat handling from the cockpit. The only decisions left for a skipper to make during the race are the political ones, such as: is it worth protesting an incident? Should we carry on racing in extreme conditions?

More important, however, is his role off the boat and before the race. As skipper he will have a final say on crew selection. If an individual is not working out or is causing upset with the rest of the crew, then it is the skipper's job to have a quiet word and suggest that perhaps he would be better off sailing on another boat. On the way out to the start, he should call the crew round for a team chat to concentrate everyone's mind on the job in hand. He can invite the navigator and/or tactician to brief the crew on the likely format and course for the race and what the wind is forecast to do. The skipper can then finish off with a few up-beat words to fire people up to get ready for the start. Too many times I have seen crews wander out to the race course, chatting, drinking coffee, talking about everything other than the race. The warning gun fires and people are still out of position and waving at their friends on other boats. Suddenly it's the start; their bodies may be there, but their minds are not. Things don't happen fast enough and 60 seconds after the start half the fleet has already gone past.

The crew needs to be fired up with adrenalin flowing before the start. Team talks are more important the bigger the boat, where some people may have only a minor job to do but it is vital they feel an integral and important part of the team so that they get their part right at the crucial time. It is also a good idea to help keep the crew on the boil or lift a flagging crew's spirits with an update during the race as to what to expect on the next leg, how you are doing at the moment and what possible result lies within reach.

Organisation at the regatta

Now you have the perfect trained crew, you are off to the season's major regatta. The planning for the event needs to be as thorough as the boat preparation so that valuable time at the venue is not wasted on maintenance or preparation that could have been done beforehand.

Make sure the boat is delivered to the regatta several days in advance, so that there is time for a lift and scrub and to allow for any delays or breakdowns on the delivery trip. Organise the rest of the crew to arrive two days before the first race to acclimatise themselves to the area, the beer and to have a couple of days practice and tune up for the local conditions.

The most successful regattas are those when the whole crew gets on well, on and off the boat. If they work hard on the water and gain some results to be proud of, and spend time together off the water, a good team spirit will develop. Such 'crew bonding' is a vital ingredient of a successful campaign. It is helped if the owner and/or skipper eats and sleeps with the crew too. Nothing breeds the 'them and us' feeling quicker than the sight of the owner heading off to his four star hotel whilst the rest of the crew are left in the overcrowded crew house.

Team jackets or polo shirts, proudly proclaiming the boat's name are a further aid to crew bonding as well as providing a psychological advantage over the opposition. Somehow, the sight of 12 guys/girls all wearing the same crew gear makes them look like they know what they are doing, compared with the boat with a scruffy assortment of crew wear. The latter look like a bunch of individuals, whereas those in team strip appear organised and efficient.

Much of the enjoyment of yacht racing comes from the close team work required to get the boat around the course in one piece and as fast as possible. The better the team you build, not only will the better the results be but so too will your enjoyment and satisfaction in the racing.

9. Attitude and Approach

Yacht racing is a sport which probably provides greater opportunity for use of the cerebral matter than many other sporting disciplines. The further you venture up the competitive ladder from national to world championship events, the harder it becomes to win races. At this level in a competitive fleet, as many as two thirds of the boats may have equal speed. Yet some sailors seem to do consistently well and in a variety of different boats.

Developing and maintaining a positive mental attitude to your racing is a vital part of the sailor's inventory and especially so at the top level. If you appreciate the role psychology can play in sailing, it is then a further tool that can be used to improve both your own and the whole crew's performance. At times you can even use a little gamesmanship to out psyche or unsettle the opposition.

The pecking order

In any fleet that sails together regularly, some form of 'pecking order' will invariably become established. This concept was first explained by Eric Twiname in his highly recommended book *Sail Race and Win* (2nd edition, Adlard Coles Nautical, 1993). Eric relates the episode when he crewed for a lady helm in the club GP 14 race. The helm, who usually finished towards the end of the fleet, was delighted when they rounded the windward mark third but immediately began to look back and speculate on how many boats would pass them on the next leg. She stopped concentrating and sailed slower as a result, subconsciously ensuring that she would soon slip back to her accustomed position in the fleet. She was already looking forward to the praise and congratulations after the race for a great first beat, but without the annoyance and antagonism of her peers who would otherwise have been displaced from their regular finishing order.

Whilst the more competitive sailor might think that if they found themselves unexpectedly at the front of the fleet, they would fight like hell to stay there, elements of Twiname's theory hold true for all of us. How many of us have crossed the finish line, having lost places in the race, but talked ourselves into a better performance. 'Well, we didn't win but we beat X and Y and they were first and second in the last race' or 'We had a better start than the winner and were well ahead of him to the first mark!'

131

Some of these observations make us feel better because although we did not win, we tell ourselves we did well during certain periods of the race. Unfortunately, yacht racing has ultimately only one measure of how good we are at it: the finishing position. Accepting the fact that the 'pecking order' theory does exist in some way in all of us is the first step in turning it around into a positive mental asset.

Learn to analyse the race from the opposite perspective. 'OK, we had a better start than the winner and the same speed upwind, so how come we let them get past?' If we do not accept that we ever make mistakes we are never going to learn from them.

When racing, I try to mentally write off the opposition around me by expecting to do better than them. If trying to spur the crew on to pass the boat just ahead I might say, 'Come on, it's old X ahead. They've only got old sails up and their hull looks filthy – we should be beating these guys easily.' I have found that if you really expect to beat a particular boat, you generally do. I suppose the incentive is the fear of losing to a boat and crew we feel is inferior to our own and the associated loss of face ashore. Psychologists may say that this is the wrong approach, but I believe it is the way most of us think and I'm sure it's best to recognise the emotion and channel it into a positive mental stimulus. It is a technique which at times you may have to talk yourself into on the race course. 'OK, so the guy to leeward is a double gold medallist, but he's going slow today, our speed is a little better so we should be ahead of him by the top mark.' The sales training consultant will tell you that if you really want to do something and you repeatedly keep telling yourself that you can, the subconscious will take over and soon it will come to pass. 'Reinforcing success', they call it in the manual!

Maybe this is a school of thought that stems from sailing singlehanded dinghies where, having no crew, you tend to talk to yourself as you go round the course. In those days I used to force myself to believe that I should expect to beat the other guy, although in reality he was often much faster. The downside of this philosophy is that if you expect to win every race you are often going to be disappointed. Instead, concentrate all your efforts on expecting to beat the boats around you and you will then naturally move up the fleet.

Peace of mind

I am only happy going into a race when I know my boat is at least as well if not better prepared than the rest. Maybe I am a perfectionist, but I tend to worry if the bottom is not clean or if we don't have the right headsail up for the wind speed. Knowing your boat is well sorted is a tremendous psychological advantage to take into a race. If I think some item of equipment is not as it should be it tends to distract my thinking during the race, often totally out of all proportion. A small lump out of the leading edge of the keel may only add up to a couple of boatlengths in a three hour race, but knowing that chip is down there on the keel when you should be trimming the mainsail can nag away at your mind and can easily result in your sailing half a knot slower or making a wrong tactical decision. The silly thing is that the simpler or more one-design the boat, the more important it seems to be to have exactly the right gear. Exchange a Laser sailor's favourite tiller extension just before a race and the chances are he will finish way below his best.

Do all you can to go into a race with the crew's mind at ease, knowing the boat is as well prepared as it is possible to be. If circumstances dictate that it isn't, try to blank it out of your mind as the gun goes and do not worry about it. Say to yourself, 'There is nothing I can do about the state of the keel now, so I am just going to forget it.'

Visualisation techniques

If you are a salesman you will know all about visualisation techniques. The Olympic sailing team psychologists use similar ideas to help their sailors improve their performance by visualising themselves accelerating off the start line, tacking on the right shifts and eventually winning the race. The sailors are also recommended to resail each race in their heads afterwards, identifying points in the race where places were lost in order to learn from these mistakes.

There are certain aspects and techniques of yacht racing which are almost impossible to teach or explain in words. The feeling you get when you pull off the perfectly judged port end start is almost indescribable. Holding the boat stationary on the line, putting the bow down at 20 seconds to go, the feel of the acceleration coming on, the crew all moving on to the rail for maximum hike, the bowman signalling the distance into the line, reaching down at full speed to that inflatable buoy at the pin end, the gun magically firing just as you think you are running out of space, and the boat squirting off the starting line. Trying to explain the timing and sequence of events to a novice helmsman is hard. It has to be come an automatic response and once you have experienced doing it right, keep reliving the experience to reinforce how it feels, so that it becomes a natural sequence of events for you.

Starting is 90 per cent experience, but it is the most difficult element of racing to practise as you need a race committee, a well set up line and 30 or so other boats to make the training realistic. Repeatedly visualising the perfect start whilst lying in bed or on the train is much easier to organise!

The visualisation techniques work equally well for other, automatic sailing reactions, such as wave technique and gust response. As a youngster sailing dinghies, I read all the books trying to figure out exactly how you were supposed to steer the boat over waves. They all talked about 'the correct wave technique', without explaining clearly enough what was required.

Some had nicely drawn diagrams of neat regular wave patterns with little arrows urging you to head up into the wave then bear off down the back of it. But what do you do in a yacht when the bow is on one wave and the rudder is buried in one two waves back, and at what exact moment do you bear off? It can also be easy to get out of phase with short, irregular waves. I sailed recently with a helmsman who had read the books and had some sort of idea of wave technique but had the procedure the wrong way around and insisted on bearing off into the face of each wave and heading up out of it. The effect of this, in heavy airs, was that the boat not only slammed into the wave but heeled over more as it bore off. The next gust would then knock the boat over further by which time there was little speed left with which to power through the wave.

The fastest way to get to windward in big waves is to luff the boat slightly as each wave meets the bow. If the bow lifts nicely over the wave without banging or slapping you know you have got it right. In order to repeat the process for the next wave it is necessary to 'pull the bow off', and bear away down the back of the wave to accelerate the boat back up to speed and to regain sufficient wind angle to be able to luff the boat again without ending up head to wind. Again, it can be a difficult technique to master especially in an irregular short chop, but the noise of the hull moving over the waves will tell you when it is right and the agonising bang and consequent slowing of the boat will make it all too obvious when you catch one wrong. Learn to listen to and concentrate on the noise the boat makes as it cuts through the waves well and splice the sound together with the visual image in your mind's eye so that you can rehearse the two together. Some helmsmen have even been known to practise driving the boat blindfold in order to develop the right feel and sound.

Psyching out the opposition

I still remember clearly the day I had my first lesson in psyching out the competition. It was during a long run against the tide at a Laser regatta at Littlehampton on the south coast. I was sitting up by the dagger board with the boat heeled over to windward, staring at the transom of the boat ahead. It was then I noticed the bung was missing out of the back of his boat. Sailing upwind the drainhole would have acted like a self-bailer but on the run in light airs there was a good chance his boat could fill up and we were a good mile or so offshore.

Should I say anything or not? If I did the guy ahead would just think I was winding him up, and if I did not he might sink. After several minutes contemplation I shouted over. 'Eh, you're not going to believe this, but I think your bung is missing.' At first he ignored me, then I could see his head start to twitch a little. There then followed a pause whilst my competitor was clearly unsure of whether he should give in to his curiosity and check the transom, or assume it was a trick and carry on. Eventually he slid to the back of the boat and took a quick glance down. At once he saw that I was telling the truth and made a desperate lunge for the drainhole to find the missing bung. In his panic he dropped the tiller, the Laser rounded up and nearly capsised. I couldn't help a quiet chuckle as I slid past, another place gained.

Just occasionally in yacht racing a situation presents itself where, by a little bluff or 'gamesmanship' it is possible to outwit the opposition and gain a few places. A good example is during the pre-start manouevres on a crowded start line. With 60 seconds to go you have reserved your place on the line and carved out a nice gap to leeward, when a boat which was squeezed over early comes reaching down on top of you. This guy is bad news. Even if he is well over the line the other boat will ruin your start by sitting on top of you and taking your wind. The answer is for the middle-man or tactician to actively dissuade the 'cowboy' from choosing to start on top of you. I find lots of loud and knowledgeable sounding shouting usually does the trick, scaring off the offender who sails off down the line to find a gap next to a less noisy boat. The key is to sound professional and authoritative so that the opposition assumes you know the rules inside-out. Obviously this works best on less experienced sailors, but it is unusual for the good guys to be the ones caught in that position. The main rule is that the whole crew should know that only one person gets involved with com-municating with other boats. Meanwhile the rest of the team, and espe-cially the helm, keep their heads down and concentrate extra hard on accelerating the boat on the lead in to the start, ignoring any shouting going on around. This is actually quite hard to do. It is very easy for the helmsman with a nice approach in to the line sorted out to be thrown by a boat barging in at the last second. He may turn around to look at the boat in the last tense seconds, start shouting at it, and turn back round only to find the other boats have sheeted in and gone for the line. His tim-ing and start will have been completely blown by a distraction at the criti-cal moment.

Similarly at mark roundings, if there is a close call for water the helm should keep his eyes on the mark whilst any discussion of rights should be handled by the tactician. Some helmsmen react badly under pressure at crowded mark roundings, so make sure you keep your man cool!

Gamesmanship

An example of how a harmless bit of gamesmanship can be used to men-tally unsettle a rival at a tense moment comes from a Dragon cham-pionship a few years ago. Heading downwind in the last race, our boat was in second place astern of a very keen young crew. They were friends of mine and I knew they would not be upset by a little lighthearted banter. As soon as the helmsman began to keep looking back at us I knew he was already a little twitched. As I was in the middle of the boat looking forward trimming the kite, I could keep my eye on them without looking away from the spinnaker too much. I kept talking to the boat in front (in a friendly manner I must stress!) asking them to hurry up and get out of our way and even to tell the helmsman that he should look where he was going. As a result they got more and more nervous and we caught right up on to their transom. Whilst they were panicking about us breathing down their necks they had missed a shift off to the left which our skipper had been quietly watching for. We gybed away and then came back into the mark a length ahead and held the lead to the finish.

Over a beer after the race I told my friends that they should not have let me put them off like that. Interestingly, the crew said they were worried with me behind them on the run because they were flying a spinnaker I had made them the year before and they were concerned that I might have judged that it was not being flown absolutely right. In truth all Dragons go at much the same speed downwind if on the same angle and wind. Because they were in front and the pressure was on, a ridiculous paranoia developed, which resulted in a very capable team sailing below their best. So be warned: never let a 'name' on board another boat get to you. Just because a sailmaker or an Admiral's Cup skipper is standing at the back of another boat does not mean that they alone can radically transform that yacht's performance. We are all guilty of falling into the trap of thinking, 'Oh, there's XYZ of XYZ Sails on that boat, they must be good'. or 'There are the guys who have just finished the Whitbread Race.' Later you see the sailmaker in the bar and he tells you what an awful day he has just had racing with a customer and his completely inexperienced crew and of all their foul-ups.

There are plenty of other little tricks that can be used in close quarters racing when there is a boat hanging onto you that you just cannot shake off. Sailing upwind on the same tack, the crew on the rail can try talking amongst themselves and pointing out some imaginary problem on the rival boat, making sure they are seen doing it. After a while, the crew on the other boat will be wondering what all the fuss is about, start looking around, lose concentration and perhaps sail slower as a result. Meanwhile, your trimmers are oblivious to what is going on, and concentrate on getting past. Other gamesmanship tips include closely tailing a rival boat throughout the pre-start, whether or not you intend to sail them away from the starting line. Needlessly tacking on top of other boats is, however, an example of gamesmanship which could easily backfire. When some boat does it to you with no obvious tactical advantage your instant reaction will tend to be to return the favour as soon as an opportunity presents itself.

When engaged in a tacking duel the 'false tack' is always worth a try to shake off a covering yacht. Tack the boat as usual a few times, calling loudly as you go. Let the covering boat think they have you cold, encouraging them to tack the instant you go. Wait until the other boat is watching you closely to go again, but this time quietly spread the word that it is to be a false tack. The trimmers move into position as usual, the helm goes down, the boat begins to head up, the covering boat goes for a tack, but as soon as you see them committed to the tack the helm throws the boat back on to the old heading. If you manage to sell the opposition a dummy they will be sailing off on the opposite tack wondering what went wrong; but you only get one chance to get it right. Once the covering yacht has seen the false tack, they will not be fooled again and will wait for you to complete the next tack before they go themselves.

In the 1983 America's Cup John Bertrand, a great believer in psychological warfare, refused to let his crew be intimidated by the army of experts and champions aboard Dennis Connor's *Liberty*. Nobody was allowed to refer to the other crew by name and on the water they were simply known as the 'Red Boat'.

Motivation

The final, most important mental factor required by a successful sailor is motivation. You have to want to win. 'Fine,' you may say, 'no problem I would love to win.' But how much do you want to win? To win a Finn Class Olympic gold medal requires complete singleminded dedication to the cause for a 2–3 years campaign. The will to win has to be fostered and nurtured and is ultimately down to each individual to develop.

It is very easy to commit yourself to a hectic season of sailing in January and then find halfway through the season that you would really rather not sail every weekend and end up dreading going to the major season's regatta. Learn to plan your events so that everyone gets a break between major races, so that by the time the next one comes along you are just beginning to miss sailing again and you turn up at the regatta hungry for action. Some people are happy to race every day of their lives, but most of us perform best if we are enjoying the sailing and really want to be there.

Most crews can find someone in their midst who can be relied upon to lift crew morale in moments of deep depression. It may be the skipper with a few stirring words of inspiration, or the bowman with some wisecrack or other. It is amazing how a good laugh amongst the crew can suddenly reduce tension and stress after a major disappointment on the race course, and mentally sets the crew up to go again.

Always remember: we are supposed to be doing it for enjoyment!

Conclusion

Writing this book has re-emphasised to me how many distinct elements go into winning a yacht race. It is far from being just a question of sailing fast and being smart. The bigger and more complex the boat the harder the task. The boat needs to be highly prepared, the rig tuned, the sails fast, the crew working as a cohesive team and the rating right before you even start the race. Thereafter it is down to the skill and experience of the crew, together with a little help from Lady Luck.

And remember that learning to lose is an important part of winning. Nobody wins every race. Some races you will lose because you made mistakes; the boat was off the pace due to the wrong set-up or sails, gear failure or just bad luck. Learning to analyse why you did not win and using that knowledge to avoid the same mistake in the future is an important step towards winning the next race. Winning a series or regatta means making fewer mistakes than everyone else in each and every race. Often a championship title will come down to a few points separating two or three yachts going into the last race. The runner up is left to rue the two places lost on the finish line in the very first race which could have won the championship.

It is important for all of us too that we show some level of improvement at each regatta we enter; be you helmsman, trimmer or bowman. Just as crucial is to grow in our understanding of why we did not win on any occasion and why the winner did. There is nothing more frustrating or dispiriting for a crew than not having a clue as to why they were slow. The uncomfortable truth may be that the sailors are just not good enough for the level of competition. But if you realise the fact and wish to do something about it, you can. The lost causes are those who consistently perform at the same mediocre level, become frustrated, change their sails, the crew and finally the boat without admitting that the heart of the problem lies a little nearer home. We all have to be realistic about our innate abilities, but the great thing about sailing is that anyone can become good at sailing with a little study and a lot of application and experience. If you look at the make up of the British Olympic team at the last few games, you will find high-flying graduate city wizz-kids, unemployed boat-builders, sailors who left school at 16 with few qualifications, accountants and professional round the world yachtsmen. The great appeal of our sport is that it combines brains, brawn and skill in an exciting cocktail.

Moving from dinghy and dayboat racing to yacht racing requires the same sailing expertise plus one additional skill: man management. The ability to work as part of a close team under a skipper does not always come naturally to some. Singlehanded sailors can find it especially hard, as can previously acknowledged small boat 'tactical experts', who are used to offering advice as and when they feel like it, even if it conflicts with the thinking of the tactician.

Last season I raced with a crew who had just completed the Whitbread Round The World Race. I was installed in the cockpit and had a few words prior to the start with the other trimmer and grinder to sort out the details of who did what. Upwind seemed simple enough but they were not very explicit as to exactly how they handled the gybes. I need not have worried. I soon realised that what I had initially taken as laid back indifference to the race was in fact quiet and studious application. I had never sailed on a boat where there was less chat. Everyone knew their job exactly and there was no need to talk through each manoeuvre beforehand or even enquire if the other guy was ready. Each time a sudden tack or gybe was called there was the grinder at my elbow or the port trimmer handing me the new sheet. After sailing 32,000 miles together they had built up a rapport that resulted in the most efficient way of handling the boat.

Looking back over the numerous regattas I have sailed in, the brightest memories come from races where the teamwork was near perfect. When everyone tries 110 per cent the boat handling is like a dream, the tactician's moves all come off, and the racing is just magic. Add a decent breeze and a little sun, some dramatic scenery and the odd first place and you begin to wonder what little else there can be in life! As one boat owner put it when trying to persuade me to race an extra day, 'John, you're a long time dead.' Get out there and enjoy it and you will be half way to winning.

Index